EIGHT THINGS *NOT* TO SAY TO YOUR TEEN

Books by William Coleman
from Bethany House Publishers

CHESAPEAKE CHARLIE SERIES
Chesapeake Charlie and the Bay Bank Robbers
Chesapeake Charlie and Blackbeard's Treasure
Chesapeake Charlie and the Haunted Ship
Chesapeake Charlie and the Stolen Diamond

DEVOTIONALS FOR FAMILIES WITH YOUNG CHILDREN
Animals That Show and Tell
Before You Tuck Me In
Getting Ready for Our New Baby
If Animals Could Talk
Listen to the Animals
My Hospital Book
My Magnificent Machine
Singing Penguins and Puffed-Up Toads
Today I Feel Like a Warm Fuzzy
Today I Feel Shy
Warm Hug Book

DEVOTIONALS FOR TEENS
Earning Your Wings
Friends Forever

BOOKS FOR ADULTS
Eight Things Not to Say to Your Teen
It's Been a Good Year
Knit Together
Measured Pace
Newlywed Book
Ten Things Your Teens Will Thank You For . . . Someday
Today's Handbook of Bible Times and Customs
What Children Need to Know When Parents Get Divorced
What Makes Your Teen Tick?

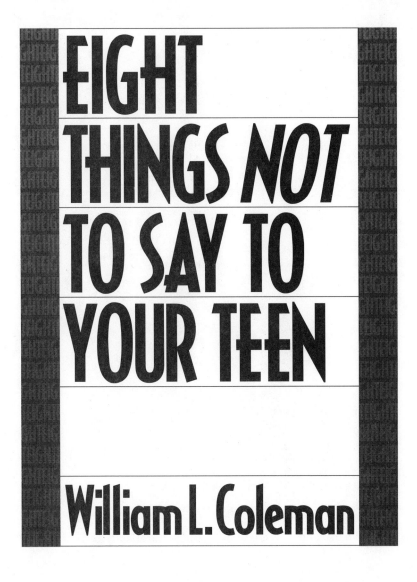

EIGHT THINGS *NOT* TO SAY TO YOUR TEEN

William L. Coleman

BETHANY HOUSE
PUBLISHERS
Minneapolis, Minnesota 55438

Published by Bethany House Publishers
A Ministry of Bethany Fellowship, Inc.
11300 Hampshire Avenue South
Minneapolis, Minnesota 55438

Printed in the United States of America

Library of Congress Cataloging-in-Publication Data

Coleman, William L.
    Eight things not to say to your teen / William L. Coleman
        p.   cm.
    1. Parenting—Religious aspects—Christianity. 2. Parent
and teenager—Religious aspects—Christianity.   3. Parent
and teenager.   4. Communication in the family.   I. Title.
BV4529.C59   1994
248.8'45—dc20   94-6776
ISBN 1–55661–404–7   CIP

Dedicated to

Eileen Bockheim

A great friend of the family
who keeps everyone around her young.

WILLIAM L. COLEMAN is the well-known author of over thirty Bethany House books on a variety of topics. Combining his experience as a pastor, researcher, writer, and speaker, he is noted for his effective communication in the area of family relationships and practical spirituality. He has been married for over thirty years and is the father of three children.

Contents

Part Three: Mixed Messages

PART ONE

How Do You Do It?

Have you ever tried to talk to someone who plays her CD three decibels above sonic boom? Have you ever started a conversation with someone watching a video of *The Creature Who Ate the Garage?* Have you ever tried to explain the new curfew hours to a person who hasn't emerged from the bathroom for forty-five minutes?

If you answered yes to any of the above, I know you. You're the parent of a teen.

And if you're the parent of a teen, you are very interested in the subject of communication—how to start it, and how to translate your teen's response, so that you, the common adult, can understand it.

Believe me, I know how you feel. One day it's like talking directly into a fan operating at full speed. The next day it's more like whispering into a paper bag and not hearing an echo in return.

Have you ever tried to talk to a sixteen-year-old boy who is dozing off at the table with his head bobbing gently into his supper plate?

Have you ever demanded to know why your daughter was out until 1:30 A.M., only to have her reply, "I think the color purple is so righteous"?

It's hard to communicate when the two participants are speaking different languages. It's even harder if one of them seems extraterrestrial.

Nevertheless, be encouraged. It *is* possible to talk to someone who wears a T-shirt that reads "Nuke the Spotted Owl." You *can* communicate with a fourteen-year-old who is in love with the school principal. You *can* transmit messages to a teen who knows more about computers, VCRs, faith, hope, and tomorrow than we may have ever dreamed.

It has been said that the first rule of medicine is to do no harm. The first rule of communicating with teens is the same. Just as important as knowing what to say is knowing what *not* to say. We adults use too many words, phrases, and cliches that shut down the avenues we need to travel in reaching our teenager. It's a lot like building our own roadblocks.

This book is designed to identify some of the verbal pitfalls we may fall into. At the same time it gives us guidelines on how to open up conversations that are more likely to result in understanding.

Take your time, listen to some good advice, and take your blood pressure pills.

1

Teens Do Listen

Do you remember what your parents told you about clean underwear, sitting up straight, *those* kind of boys, parked cars, religion, and politics? Of course you do. You still quote them—twenty, thirty, or even forty years later.

We remember the wise things, the silly sayings, the dumb ideas. We can recall volumes.

I remember entering the drive-through at Wendy's and ordering a quarter-pounder. In case you don't know (as I didn't), Wendy's doesn't make a quarter-pounder. Our three teens in the backseat laughed until tears rolled down their cheeks. Laughed? How about roared, screamed, bellowed, shouted, and snorted.

"Wasn't that clever," you might say. "What fun-loving kids." Today when we get together with them as adults, all hovering in their twenties, they still tell this same story. And they roar, fall off chairs, cackle, spit food, and spray coffee at the memory of this ancient tale.

Young people hear what you say. They listen.

They remember. And they will digest their parents' words all of their lives.

Make Sure You Say Something

As children shuffle through the adolescent years, make a mental note of how often they quote their parents to their friends. In my hearing, our daughter, Mary, told some innocent soul: "Be careful. Don't add too much water. My dad says you can do more harm from over-watering a plant than from under-watering it."

I said that? What do I know about plants? And my daughter was quoting me like I had invented the tree.

What else do they quote to their friends? Here are a few:

- "Dad said he knew he was in love within the first two weeks."
- "She said she went to bed and cried when she took her first college exams. Can you imagine? My mom?"
- "Mom always said smoking was one of the toughest habits to break."
- "Dad says you could chip a tooth."
- "Mom felt very strongly about abortion."
- "I know how my dad feels about capital punishment."
- "Don't you know parking lots are some of the most dangerous places to drive?"
- "Mom says if you want to find happiness you need to serve God."
- "A promise is a promise is a promise."
- "Pick a lane, any lane."
- "Train's leaving."

Everything from profound to mundane to silly

to practical to puzzling. They listen. They may not obey, but apparently they hear a lot of what we say. Some things they need to sift through, weigh, even reject, but the first step to learning is hearing.

Frustrated parents say, "What's the use? They don't listen to me anyway."

But they do. A recent study about who uses drugs and why came to this conclusion: Of the young people surveyed, those adolescents whose parents have told them not to abuse drugs and alcohol are less likely to do so. In the cases where parents have said nothing about the use of drugs and alcohol, the young people were more likely to use them.

How profound! If we tell our teens not to use substances, they might still use them. But, if we tell them not to, they are *less* likely to do so.

We aren't always talking to a brick wall. Sometimes it just feels like it.

Speaking up *is* worth the effort. It pays to put data into a teenager's information bank. That's called communication.

There's No Room for Doubt

Two things have always been true:

- We need to talk with our teens.
- Our talking to them does have an impact, even if we think it doesn't.

As parents we need to be encouraged to keep communicating. We also need to learn ways to do it better. How do we talk to teens? What do we say? When do we say it? How do we become good listeners? Adults who do not listen are not good communicators.

There is little hope for parents who clam up and give up. Once we feel like "there is no sense in talking," we have entered the danger zone. Even when you become frustrated and humiliated you must muster up the courage to keep the communication lines open. Remember, there is a right time and a correct way, but the main thing is to keep talking.

Get Rid of Your Negatives

All of us have our reasons for why we stop talking to our teen. We repeat them over and over to ourselves, hoping the excuses are reasonable and valid.

- "It all goes in one ear and out the other."
- "It's like talking to a brick wall."
- "I'm just wasting my breath."
- "What's the use?"
- "She'll just do whatever she wants anyway."
- "He never listens to me."
- "You can't tell him anything."
- "I talk until I'm blue in the face."
- "She doesn't think I know anything."

Do you have another favorite excuse for no longer trying to communicate? If we expect to promote dialogue with our teen (or even a monologue), we have to quit trying to convince ourselves that the effort is hopeless.

All of these statements, and others like them, are simply wrong. Teens *do* hear what we say and it does register, even if it doesn't look like it. If we keep rehearsing these negative phrases, we will talk ourselves out of talking.

Where We Get Confused

Even if it goes in one ear and out the other, it is still our responsibility to put information in the one ear. Whether a teen shrugs it off, refuses to accept it, or disobeys what we say is entirely another matter.

We confuse two separate actions: our provision of information; and our teen's response to that information.

When a teen moves in and lives with her boyfriend we say that she refused to listen.

That's false. She no doubt did listen. She may even have agreed with you. But she didn't do what you said. Every rational parent must separate the giving of information and the teen's response to that information.

We would make a grave mistake if we decided, "She isn't going to do what I say, so there is no sense in talking to her." On the contrary, she needs information in order to make choices. If we withhold information she becomes morally deprived. No parent can afford to leave their teen without a value system (even if the system is rejected).

Family Proverbs

Part of our value system was handed down to us by the people who raised us—our parents, grandparents, even aunts and uncles. These values may include those from the Scriptures or Christian teaching passed down through our families or the church. In any case the value system we have received is the one we hand down to our children. If you read the book of Proverbs, it is obvious that the author, Solomon, was doing this in writing. He was anxious that his own children receive proper instruction so that they would not experience harm to themselves, or hurt anyone else. To pass on our values is the noblest of causes.

Each of us has a *code of ethics* and a *set of beliefs*. These make up our *system of values*. Our primary role in raising a family, along with providing food and shelter, is to pass along these proverbs—our basic beliefs about right and wrong—to our children. No teen should be able to honestly say, "I don't know how my parents feel about lying, stealing, God, money, sex, love, and crime." If they haven't a clue as to how we feel, we have deprived them of a moral base.

A Code of Ethics

Your family's code of ethics is what you consider right and wrong, good and bad. It is the discipline of moral duty or obligation.

For example, it is wrong to cheat on taxes, insurance claims, or school exams. We teach these ethics within our families to help establish a moral foundation. It takes years to teach, demonstrate, and instill the large array of ethics that are considered vital for a healthy human being to operate in society.

Ethics include the way we treat others. Without good ethics we become greedy, self-centered, and isolated from the people around us.

A Set of Beliefs

What do we believe about God and His Son—Jesus Christ—the Bible, and eternity? We need to share that faith with the people we love. Otherwise our teens are left as blank slates waiting for some-one else to write on them.

Imagine your teen taking a faith test about you, his parents. He or she is handed a list of twenty questions about your faith. These might include:

1. My parents believe Jesus Christ is _____
2. My parents believe the Bible to be the infal-lible Word of God.
3. My parents believe the way to live forever is to _____
4. My parents would cheat on a tax return ____ Yes ____ No ____ Maybe

How close would your teen come to writing down the right answers—what you would have written? Or does your teen not have the faintest idea what you believe? They should know. And it doesn't all come by osmosis.

A System of Values

A value system based upon the Scriptures is the best foundation we can provide our children, arming them with guidelines and the ability to make wise decisions. Woe to the teenager who has had few examples of biblical values both by word and deed.

Because verbal communication is the key to passing on vital information to our teens, our goal should be to find the best ways to connect with young people. Especially the ones in our own homes.

2

Teen Panic Attacks

A hurricane has hit the house. Or so it seems.

Your daughter breezes in and announces in a frantic voice, "Everybody's going to the party!" She's wringing her hands and her face shows desperation, defying any halt to her plans.

"What party?" you, the shell-shocked mother, asks, trying to remain calm and casual.

"It's at Lani's cousin's house. Don't worry; it's just the good kids that are going to be there. I have to leave in less than an hour!"

"You haven't eaten supper. Slow down and let's talk about this."

"I can't. I just barely have time to shower and change clothes. And I've got to call Lani. Don't worry. There'll be plenty to eat at the party. We'll talk about it when I get home, I promise. Pleeese, Mom. I've got to go."

What is going on here? You feel the panic vibes and somehow you are left without details, without vital information. It's called Teen Urgency. The first time it rocks your household you may be sent reeling, your ears ringing, your reflexes rattling. It takes a few minutes to figure out what it is, but eventually you recover and pull yourself together.

Lock the doors. Close the shutters. Bring in the lawn chairs. Wait a minute! It's not a storm, your teenager is just home again.

No Time to Talk

If this happens at your house, don't panic. Everything is perfectly normal. The typical teen will insist that there is
- no time to talk
- no time for details
- no time to think it over
- no time to call anyone
- no reason to be concerned.

To the teen this is an emergency, and he expects his parents, as "old and out of it" as they may be, to recognize that fact.

Our daughter used to come home and say, "I need to leave in an hour to go to a movie in Grand Island."

To which I would reply blankly, "You need to go where?"

"You heard me, Dad," she would snap back boldly. "You're just stalling."

Stalling? Maybe. She had no patience with my patience. She wanted an automatic yes so she could get moving without delay.

I had to admire her efficiency even if I was taken aback by her boldness.

My response was usually, "If I have to answer right now, the answer is no." Only then did she gear down to a negotiating pace.

"Hey, no hurry," she would assure me. "Take

your time. I know we can work this out. No big deal.''

Panic Attacks

To most teens there are few things as important as *right now*. They may want college, a career, and other prizes that lie in the future, but they suffer from adolescent panic attacks. Suddenly, without warning, they become overwhelmed with the immediate.

Teens aren't joking when they say they have to have it *now*. Their minds, their bodies, their social setting tell them that their world hinges on what happens in the next three or four hours. It's almost as if their very lives depended on it.

A teenage boy from Kansas said he had the whole process down to a science. He would saunter into the family room and calmly announce where he was going. Without waiting for a reply he would systematically add

- there will be no drugs
- there will be no alcohol
- there will be no sex
- my room is cleaned up
- my homework is finished
- I will get up on time tomorrow.

He knew exactly what the checklist would be, so he tried to speed up the interrogation with these statements. His parents were under constant pressure to devise new and probing questions in an attempt to slow down the whirlwind process.

Yes, Patience Is a Virtue

What does the Bible tell us about learning to calm down and wait?

1. "A man's wisdom gives him patience . . ." (Proverbs 19:11).
2. "A patient man has great understanding, but a quick-tempered man displays folly" (Proverbs 14:29).
3. "But the fruit of the Spirit is love, joy, peace, patience . . ." (Galatians 5:22).

These references suggest that it takes time to learn patience, and teens have little experience with this process. It may be unreasonable to expect a young person to acquire instant patience (which is an oxymoron, anyway).

Therefore, don't become angry over something most teens are poorly equipped to do; in fact, you can expect impatience in your teen while you are being patient with him or her.

Enjoy Their Spontaneity

When we admire young people, what is it that we particularly appreciate about them?

- Their high energy
- Their ability to enjoy themselves
- Their intense involvement in a given activity
- Their spontaneity
- Their creativity
- Their sense of curiosity
- Their quest for adventure

These are some of the reasons why youth workers like to be around teens. Ironically, they are some of the same reasons why parents are frightened of their teenagers. *The same traits we admire in other teens may be the ones we distrust and fear in our own teens.* We enjoy them from afar but we might be threatened by those characteristics within our own walls.

A teen's destructive urgency is simply the flip side of his or her constructive urgency.

Our goal as parents should not be to destroy our teens' sense of the immediate, but rather to help them distinguish between the valid urgencies and the less than urgent.

Intensity is not bad in itself. When we see a busload of teens leaving to feed the poor in Mexico, we admire their adventure and sensitivity to the needs of the less fortunate. We cheer those who volunteer to work in the inner cities. The catch is to channel a teenager's intensity or enthusiasm rather than trying to extinguish it.

Conflict of Passions

Where parents get into deep trouble is when their own deep passions conflict with their teen's desires. What a parent may see as extremely important can be insignificant and even petty to the teenager (and maybe it really is, by any standard).

Adults need to sift out their driving forces and ask which ones are worth fighting for. Ask as a marine might, "Is this a hill worth dying on?"

Are parental goals good simply because they are the goals of the parent? Adults should be mature enough to reevaluate what is important to the family as a whole, carefully weighing their goals and regulations against their teen's desires and wishes.

How to React to Panic Attacks

Plan ahead as to how you will deal with these sudden adrenalin rushes. The better prepared you are, the saner you will be when your teen comes flying through the door.

1. *Discuss* with your teen your perspective when he or she approaches you in a panic. Understand also that impulses are strong forces in a teen's life and try to respect them.

2. *Confess.* Sometimes a parent insists on his own way and wants it immediately. Admit that you and your teen may suffer from the same affliction.

3. *Explain.* When a teenager wants something this minute, the parent doesn't have enough time to weigh the situation. Afraid of making a decision she will regret, the parent needs sufficient time to ruminate and digest all the factors.

You might say to your teen, "Please don't rush me, because under too much pressure I make big mistakes. Occasionally I may be able to answer you quickly when something special comes up on the spur of the moment, but usually you will get a more favorable answer when that extra-special, super-fantastic occasion comes up and you give me some time to think about it. I may even think to myself, *She is not acting on impulse; this must be something good that she has thought through. Of course I can let her go.*

And your teen may think, *What an all-together parent!*

It takes time and consistency, but it can be done. Teens can learn how to control their panic attacks and how to approach parents calmly and with a little time to think. Soon they will realize that if they do it correctly, they will greatly increase the odds of having their request granted.

Parents do their teens a service by teaching them how to present their case in the best possible manner.

In our family, June was the impulse queen. She had a great deal to do and thought she couldn't always give us adequate warning, which resulted in a lot of "no's."

Eventually family members shared their own experiences with June on how to best approach her old dad.

"Warn him three days in advance," her sister Mary said. "That way he won't feel like it's a big surprise when something happens."

"After you ask him," suggested brother Jim, "don't bug him every day about it."

"And never when he first comes in the door," her mother reminded. "When he gets home from work, his answer is almost always no to anything. Let him settle in, eat supper, take off his shoes. When his shoes are off, it's easy to talk him into almost anything."

June didn't do everything correct the next day or the next week, but our conversations improved. Soon she learned the art of controlling her impulses, and began to see more "Wait-and-see's" and "No's" turn into "Yes's."

That's fair, isn't it? Tell your teenager what system works. The goal isn't to frustrate. It's for everything to move as smoothly as possible—even during a teen attack.

A parent's role is not to throw cold water on a teen's plans and desires, but to take time, weigh the options, and come to an agreeable solution.

3

Cultural Wars

"Let me tell you about my teen," a mother said to me. "I don't like what she wears. I don't like her attitude. I don't like her friends. I can't stand her music. She's developed a trashy mouth."

"What do you enjoy about your teenager?" I responded.

"That's the problem. I can't think of one thing."

This mother isn't entirely unusual. She wants to talk to her teen, help her teen, and change her teen because she can't think of anything she likes about the girl. Just the fact that she has approached another adult about it means she would like to come to some understanding with her child.

But from this posture it is almost impossible for the two to share any meaningful communication. The mother can still give orders, issue commands, and state facts, but heartfelt give and take is unlikely. There have to be some positives.

It's hard to admit some of us simply don't "like" teenagers. What ogre could be opposed to youth's brightness, vitality, and vigor? The fact is, many adults are, and this includes some parents of teens.

You may feel like opening a window and shouting to the world, "I can't stand teens!" PHEW! Now, do you feel better?

The Giant Barrier

I met a man who worked with teenagers in a group home. A tight, almost brittle person, this man thought his task in life was to determine what young people wanted to do, and then *keep them from doing it.*

He believed teens should act like adults. His job was to deprive them of their culture and make them comply to his.

People like this are more common than we think.

"I became a mom to raise children," said one mother. "I didn't sign on to raise teenagers. I always knew I was going to hate that part of it."

That's the giant barrier right there. Some of us insist that we don't know what to say to a teen or how to say it, and whatever comes up with them we are going to hate. But, the fact is, it's all but impossible to have meaningful dialogue with someone we don't like in the first place. We have a preconceived idea of how it's going to turn out.

Parental Culture

Most of us consider our culture or daily habits a prized possession. However, we might not realize how we value it until someone challenges it. A parent, for example, might like to drink a cup of coffee and read the newspaper every morning. He or she probably doesn't think much about it until someone makes fun of it.

Let a teen say, "Oh, I don't see how you can stand to drink that stuff," or, "There isn't anything worth reading about in the paper, is there?" and you'll find out how much you cherish your daily routine.

Let a young person degrade a parent's music, clothing, food, habits, friends, car, or favorite television show and see how defensive the parent becomes. Adults tend to believe that what they like or do is "right." They may also tend to think that what a teen likes or does is automatically "wrong."

But culture isn't a matter of right or wrong. Culture is a matter of preference and learned behavior.

If a parent objects to her teen's behavior, she must stop and ask herself why she objects. In the case of choice of music, for instance, the objection cannot simply be because the music is different. Are the lyrics immoral, or is the problem strictly cultural? Parents have no right to be upset merely because they don't prefer their teen's style of music.

When it comes to an honest difference of opinion, shouldn't the teen have as much freedom to choose as the adult? If not, we are saying adult culture is "more acceptable" than teen culture. Young people will most likely rebel under this system.

Teenage Culture

The life of a teen is at once exciting, scary, exhilarating, and depressing. One of the major reasons for so many highs and lows is because the teen lives on the cutting edge of change. They are sampling tomorrow's technology, tomorrow's government, tomorrow's work skills, tomorrow's humor, tomorrow's health risks, tomorrow's relationships, tomorrow's education, tomorrow's adventures. Since change is coming so rapidly, their heads are spinning as they try to absorb all that's affecting their lives.

Teenagers today will see far more cultural changes than their parents saw in their youth. Their minds have to process new information as rapidly as possible because there's more coming and it keeps changing. Unfortunately, they may face this cutting edge with less support, emotional stability, and moral training than the generation before them.

With all the turmoil they face on a daily basis, the last thing teens need is a continuous battle with parents over purely cultural differences.

Paul's Principle

When Paul wrote the book of Romans, parent/teen conflicts may not have been at the top of his list of concerns. But the apostle laid down some guidelines that could well be applied to these cultural wars.

His principle is that if one person can freely eat meat while another thinks he can eat only vegetables, leave both of them alone (Romans 14:1–8). Each might be correct. Who are we to judge?

Too often we as adults let our egos get in the way. Don't stop a teen unless you are sure he or she is heading in the wrong direction.

Removing the Barriers

Take a piece of paper and pen and pretend you're a lawyer. Make three columns at the top of the paper: Good points, Neutral points, Bad points.

Now begin listing the characteristics of your teen in the column where you think they belong. Write down everything from his or her hairstyle to choice in friends. Is your teen's language rude and insulting? Does he show great potential in academics? Is her music preference a neutral point with you, or something you want to change?

The next step is to work on the column shift. Where are we being unfair?

We need a lot of help from the Lord on this one. We also need to talk to other parents, friends, teens, youth workers, and others. Do we have some traits, habits, or characteristics in the wrong column?

Is it time to move hairstyle and clothes to the good column?

Is it time to transfer friends from the bad column to the neutral one?

Or is it time to move friends from the neutral column to the bad column?

Now go over your list and write the letter G next to each habit that you think will cause God to stop loving that teen or give up on him. Next, go over the list a second time and write the letter P beside each trait or action that will cause you, the parent, to stop loving that teen or give up on him. Take your time with this. Be honest and fair.

The goal is to reach the place where we begin to share the mind of God toward our teenager.

The Edge of Tomorrow

Teens and their parents will always live in contrast because their perspectives are different.

Parents live with forty years of history behind them. Teens live on the edge of tomorrow. Adults tend to preserve what they have known. Teens are more likely to experiment with the future. Adults are fixed on what has been. Teens are curious over what might be.

It's much like sitting in different sections of the same bus. Parents sit in the back and enjoy the familiar scenery. Teens crowd up near the driver's seat to get an early glimpse of what lies ahead. Dialogue begins when we learn to appreciate why each person has chosen to sit where they do.

If we are to appreciate young people, we must first accept their quest for the future. They want and need to try new things. As long as their search for tomorrow isn't evil, criminal, or sinful, don't stand in their way. Learn to enjoy their enthusiasm for a new life.

4

The Silent Scream

The difference between fifth grade and sixth is obvious to any teacher. If you ask the students in the fifth grade to read their papers aloud, hands shoot up like rockets. Ask them to do the same in the sixth grade and it's instant stony silence.

Most sixth graders will sit motionless, staring at the floor, their shoes, or the backs of their hands.

Something happens around this age that causes the pre- or early teen to lose all verbal skills. Yesterday they talked like auctioneers. Today they have become mummies—bound, gagged, and muted.

Jason's vocabulary loss lasted for three years. Though never verbally proficient, the twelve-year-old did have a tongue and a working knowledge of the English language. The day after his thirteenth birthday, Jason dropped into mute silence and stayed there until he was old enough to drive.

The sudden change was devastating to his parents. They were convinced he was either on drugs, had a brain tumor, or was trying to make contact with alien creatures. Since he never spoke and only gave limited hand motions, how was anyone to know what was transpiring in this vacant lot called "personality"?

Communication Dropout

There are two essentials to communication: a transmitter and a receiver. In this case the receiver just conked out. The batteries went dead. The transmitter (commonly known as the parent) kept squawking endlessly into the night, but each message seemed lost on the airwaves.

The time will come when you will be tempted to call 911 and ask for the jaws-of-life to pry open your teen's mouth. Don't give in and make that call.

What Ties Their Tongues?

Most of the ropes that tie their tongues are of the same variety that tied our own tongues as teens. See how many you recognize.

1. *Fear.* Teenagers basically fear four things:
   a. themselves
   b. peers
   c. adults/parents
   d. God

Their days and nights are filled with serious, adolescent apprehension. These are not insignificant fears. Sometimes they border on stark terror.

2. *Change.* A teen changes so rapidly he becomes a stranger even to himself. He isn't sure who he is becoming.

   a. His/her body is changing.

    b. His/her mental process is changing.
    c. His/her opportunities are changing.
    d. His/her choices are changing.
    e. His/her responsibilities are changing.
    f. His/her family/world is changing.

Too much is unstable. No one can be in the middle of all this and expect to sort it all out alone. A teen can become bewildered.

3. *Trial and error.* Teens frequently don't know what they think, how they feel, what they want, or where they want to be. Still in the process of discovery, they are hesitant to voice views that are still being formed or discuss interests that are still being developed.

Ask a young person how she feels about abortion and she may not be prepared to toss her opinion out on the table for everyone to see. Yet ask her about the city curfew and she might jump at the opportunity to talk.

4. *Criticism.* No one likes to be attacked. Teens are unlikely to feed their feelings to the wolves. If they believe their parents or any other adult is going to pounce on their opinions and tear them to shreds, he or she is not prone to speak up.

Inching into the adult world, they aren't sure how to operate in the market of ideas. If they blurt out, "I think marijuana should be legalized," is the ceiling going to cave in? Will their parents ground them, lecture them, become suspicious of their activities? If they have ventured their opinion and been chided because of it, they will be reluctant to express their feelings again.

How to Melt the Ice

When someone is not talking, he is still communicating. The message is, "I refuse to explain what I am thinking at this moment." What they *aren't* saying is the reason they aren't talking.

Parents naturally want to know. "How can I make my teen talk?"

Wrong question! Change it to something like this: "How do I create an atmosphere in which my teen feels free to talk?"

Or, "How do I remove the obstacles that frighten my teen?"

Or, "How do I open myself up to accept whatever my teen has to say?"

Those questions put us into the ice-melting business. But no matter how "talker friendly" we might make our home, our teen could still stonewall us. Nevertheless, our task is to create an environment where conversation is easy and welcome.

How to Create the Right Environment

Go over this checklist and see what is true of your home atmosphere. Perhaps some changes are necessary.

1. *Don't dominate the conversation.* Teens are given a green light when they hear their parents talk in a free, relaxed style, with natural pauses for response. The red light comes on when they have to interrupt in order to get a word in edgewise.

Talk. Listen. Be patient. Be objective. Be silent when necessary.

2. *Be shockproof.* Try not to turn purple if your teen brings up AIDS, condoms, crack, gangs, or a co-ed overnight camp-out. Remain seated if they ask to go bungee jumping, hang gliding, or want cash to take sword-swallowing lessons.

An open line on a radio talk show means you

can call in and discuss any subject. Teens need an open forum where they can speak their minds when they are in the mood, and be heard.

At our house, our teens asked if they were planned conceptions or accidents. After choking in my napkin, I was able to answer very calmly.

3. *Allow time.* Supply plenty of free, relaxed, flexible time in which to exchange conversation and ideas. Teens don't talk to harried, hurried, frazzled parents who have more "important" things to do. Develop interests where you and your teen are together for extended periods. Young people are far more likely to open up during unofficial, unstructured time slots.

4. *Be transparent.* Share your feelings as an adult and your memories as a teen. Talk about old boyfriends, girl friends, good times at school, anxieties, peer pressure, and other experiences. This helps you to identify with your teens and gives them permission to take risks with you.

Describe some of your mistakes and nutty behavior. Teens enjoy discovering the human side of their parents. But don't major on your trouble-making days. If that's all they ever hear, that's all they will want to emulate.

5. *Grease the conversation.* Someone said that the art of psychology is simply to repeat the client's last sentence: "You say your mother took your teddy bear away?" With that spark the client will go on speaking for another ten minutes.

It works with your teen. Repeat what he or she just told you: "She dropped out of school? Do you know why?" or, "He's not living at home? Was there some problem there?"

Don't simply sit and wait for your teen to finish talking. Jump in just enough to let him know you are with him in the conversation and that he has your rapt attention.

Toss out the attitude "How will I make my teen talk?" Usually that only drives her further into the ground. You wouldn't stand in front of a prairie dog hole and shout until the frightened animal came out. The longer and louder you insist it appear, the less likely it will be to emerge.

Settle down. Lie back. The prairie dog just might stick its head out and say something.

5

The Role of Storyteller

One of the most regrettable aspects of our hurried society is the lost practice of family storytelling. Who today takes the time to share tales about parents, uncles, aunts, grandparents, and even shirttail relatives? More than mere entertainment, stories can be used to enrich our children, providing them with a sense of roots, family connection, and even a valuable source of self-counseling at a time when they need it most.

Not long ago I told our children the story of my Aunt Mildred. A terrific Christian woman, she has always served as an inspiration to our family.

A woman of modest means, Mildred sought to be faithful to the Lord. For years she tithed consistently of all she had, even when times were tough. Then one day Aunt Mildred became convinced that tithing was an Old Testament rule, not something that applied today.

Consequently, she gave up tithing and made a pact with the Lord. From then on she would only give as she felt led. If she saw someone in need, this cheerful octogenarian would send a few dollars in their direction.

Mildred followed this new scheme for a year. Steadily she contributed to needs here and there as she became aware of them. At the end of twelve months, Mildred added up how much she had given away. It came out to ten percent of her income!

Either by law or by grace, Aunt Mildred couldn't resist the spirit of generosity.

These are the stories teenagers need to hear. Aunt Mildred didn't lead the battle at Normandy or build the Eiffel Tower (though she may have been able to do either), but she did emulate Christ's selflessness and generosity. It's a human story. It's a spiritual story. It's a story about values. It's a story that encourages and even enables.

Each of us probably has a closet full of tales like this. If they are told in the right way, at the right time, they can become sources for our children to draw on as they develop their own character, integrity, and a sense of belonging.

An Easy Way to Educate

Paul Welter calls stories "a way to learn without trying."[1] He reminds us that logical, sequential, analytical learning takes a lot of work. Stories, on the other hand, put pleasant surprise into learning.

When my daughter June was contemplating marriage, she asked me how long I had dated her mother before I knew I loved her, and I was honest

---

[1] Paul Welter, *Learning from Children*; P.O. Box 235, Kearney, NE 68848, p. 45.

with her: two weeks. I knew June wasn't asking to hear my theories on love at first sight (though I have plenty of theories), so I told her about our first dates.

I drew word pictures about the Chinese food, the walks by the Jefferson Memorial, the cherry blossoms, the paddle boat rides, and the European restaurant complete with violins. The stories of our experiences and feelings sounded very similar to June's, and eventually she went on to marry Phil.

In *The Living Reminder* [2] Henri Nouwen tells us that one of the remarkable qualities of stories is that they provide space. We can walk around a story and look for a place to connect. We can sit down, stand up, and ask with whom we identify. Stories are not oppressive or manipulative. A story can inspire, encourage, set examples, offer choices.

Normally I can't repeat what a minister said in his sermon, but regularly I can recall the stories he told. I connect with people and events far more easily than with platitudes and directives.

In Christ's story of the Prodigal Son there are several places to plug into. We can identify with the father, the son, or the brother. We can also see ourselves as the opposite of the characters. We might see ourselves as one particular individual at a given time but not at another time. Stories offer us flexibility in our search for practical help.

The greatest teacher who ever lived was a storyteller. There are dozens of stories recorded in the Bible, called parables, that Jesus Christ told. Much of what we have learned from the Scriptures sticks with us because we can picture the characters and events in our minds. Our role as parents should

---

[2]Henri Nouwen, *The Living Reminder* (New York: The Seabury Press, 1981), pp. 65, 66.

also include the important and valuable task of the family storyteller.

A parent's willingness to tell stories opens the door for his teen to do the same. If we lock the safe that contains our experiences, the teen is far more likely to lock up his own.

Give Teens Time and Space to Tell Their Own Stories

Young people have stories they need to tell. Their experiences are not necessarily high adventures, but they depict life.

The adults to whom they are most likely to tell their stories are the ones who tell stories themselves and who enjoy listening to others.

Story accessibility means

- The listener is not in a rush.
- The listener enjoys stories.
- The listener doesn't have to hear a great moral.
- The listener is willing to let the story take its own path.
- The listener doesn't think he or she has heard it all.
- The listener likes new twists and surprises.
- The listener doesn't feel superior.
- The listener hears with his face and heart, not just his ears.
- The listener doesn't judge the characters for their actions.
- The listener loves new adventures.

Fill the Treasure Chest

The sooner we begin supplying our children with stories, the better. But when your teen breaks curfew and shows up at 3:00 A.M., it's no time to launch into a story about someone who broke curfew and suffered dire consequences. Stories are best told (and retold) in a relaxed setting over a period of time. It's much like eating plums. An occasional one is great, but a dozen at one sitting could dull the senses.

Reach back into your memory's treasure chest and pull out the events that amused, entertained, and amazed you as a youth. Add to those some recent stories about courage, faith, and adventure. Even stories about silliness, lessons learned, and wonders seen.

Don't expect every tale to be greeted with wide eyes. Simply tell it and let it float. Someday when you least expect it, your teen may say to you, "That's when I decided I had better do something about it. When I remembered what you told me about what Uncle Lance did."

You'll be glad the treasure chest was full.

When possible, every child should know about the "good stock" they came from. Even in families whose pictures hang regularly in the post office, there are some good people and fine stories to be told. In the famous bank robbery at Coffeyville, Kansas, the Dalton brothers were shot up and imprisoned. But at the same time another Dalton brother served as a U.S. Marshall. There are always some uplifting stories to tell among the police records.

We all have tales that are ready-made to bolster a sagging soul, stories that heal and strengthen.

Five Don'ts for Family Storytelling

1. Don't tell stories that are heavy-handed and sharply pointed. Blunt, heavily moralistic stories

are deadly. They leave no space or breathing room. The best stories allow the hearers to find themselves in the tale.

2. Don't pull out a story like a sword when your teen is in trouble. Load up the treasure chest beforehand.

3. Restrict the number of "bad" stories about yourself. Tell a couple of stories about how you or someone in the family messed up or got into trouble—and how you got out. But don't make these your steady selection.

4. Keep the stories short. Teens have a *very* short attention span.

5. Don't stumble over details. If you don't know what year or what kind of cake it was, keep moving. If the storyteller keeps correcting the details, the listener's eyes start to glaze over.

Five Do's of Family Storytelling

1. Tell stories while the sun shines. Some stories should be told in hospital waiting rooms or in jail cells, but most should be told before the hard times come. Store them up so the teen can reflect on them later.

2. Enhance family members. When possible, tell uplifting, enriching, satisfying tales about the good deeds of relatives. Young people need to feel they are connected to "decent" folk. It makes them feel decent about themselves.

3. Retell tales. It is risky to tell a story over and over but it needs to be done. If you tell it as they grow up, when they reach college age they may tell it back to you.

A good story, well told, deserves to be repeated.

4. Choose the appropriate time. Never say, as

your teen heads out the door, "Oh, I've got a great story for you." The story is then an intrusion. Aim for open, friendly, peaceful situations when stories can really count.

5. Listen to their stories. Nothing is as insufferable as a person who has a ton of tales to tell and no time to listen to others. You want your teens to talk. Let them.

When a youth begins to share her story, block out everything else and listen one-hundred percent. This opportunity may not come often.

A story is an excellent device for teaching creative problem-solving. That's a major reason why we tell and retell Bible stories. We learn how God worked in the lives of people as they faced rebellion, moral choices, illness, sibling rivalry, theft, incest, adultery, prejudice, hate, fear, and a great deal more. Those pictures and images affect our behavior most of our lives.

When a ninth-grader sits in class and wonders whether or not to cheat on his history test, it would be great if he had a little help. The memory of an old family story about Aunt Linda who refused to cheat on her income tax might supply just the moral courage he needs.

Open Bible Stories

Often, when adults tell Bible stories, they tend to moralize over the characters and make applications. Stories told this way allow no space for the hearer to walk around.

When sharing stories about Jonah, Samson, Hannah, or Esther with teens, we need to open up the characters. Ask the young people why these characters did what they did. Ask how they felt.

Ask what alternatives they had. With which characters do the teens most closely identify?

Reintroduce storytelling as an anchor to help hold your young people on firm ground.

Why Don't We Listen?

The refusal or inability to listen has many causes. Teens accuse adults of never listening, and there is some truth to their charge. Sometimes we don't listen.

Let's look at ourselves as parents and ask why we don't listen. Below are twenty reasons why an adult might not keep his or her ears open when a teen starts talking.

Read each statement and then score yourself on a scale of one to five. One means you never feel this way, five indicates this is very true of what you think or feel. (Grade yourself on how strongly you agree with each statement.)

1. I don't believe what they say.   1 2 3 4 5
   Why listen to teens when they
   exaggerate and don't tell the truth
   anyway?

2. I consider all talk back talk.   1 2 3 4 5
   Young people shouldn't reply when
   they are told what to do.

3. I know what took place.   1 2 3 4 5
   What is the point of dragging it out?

4. They won't say what you want to
   hear.   1 2 3 4 5
   Since the teen isn't likely to admit
   he is wrong, there is no point in
   discussing it.

5. I distrust discussion.   1 2 3 4 5
   Right is right and wrong is wrong,
   so why talk about it?

6. Other parents don't listen.   1 2 3 4 5
   It is foolish to listen to excuses
   when other parents insist they
   don't.

7. I feel defensive.   1 2 3 4 5
   I hate being challenged because I'm
   not sure I can defend what I said.

8. Talking is stalling.   1 2 3 4 5
   Teens are trying to bluff by talking
   when they really need to admit their
   mistakes.

9. I had no role model for it.   1 2 3 4 5
   My parents didn't listen to me and I
   turned out fine.

10. It's a waste of time.   1 2 3 4 5
    I don't think discussion is
    important.

11. How a teen feels isn't really the
    issue.   1 2 3 4 5
    Obedience is the key, not emotions.

12. Teens don't understand authority.   1 2 3 4 5
    Soldiers don't stand around
    discussing the general's orders.

13. I need to display authority.   1 2 3 4 5
    It's important that I look like I'm in
    control.

14. No one listens to me.   1 2 3 4 5
    People out in the *real world* don't
    care what I think; that's the way life
    is.

15. Listening will weaken my teenager.   1 2 3 4 5
    He/she will end up being a touchy-
    feely person instead of one who is
    tough and steady.

16. I already have the answer.   1 2 3 4 5
    Curfew is 11:00 P.M.; what's to talk
    about?

17. Teens should be seen and not heard.   1 2 3 4 5
    I want to see them diligently
    working, not trying to negotiate
    their way out of something.

18. I have a busy schedule.   1 2 3 4 5
    I have more pressing things to do.

19. Teens appreciate rules that don't
    waiver.   1 2 3 4 5
    Young people want boundaries set
    for them.

20. I know what it's like to be a teen.   1 2 3 4 5
    It's only been twenty years, times
    haven't changed that much.

Now, add up your points.

If you have 100 points, you need to use your ears more often.

If you have 60 points, you are grappling with reality.

If you have only 10 points, it may be time to

stop listening and speak up!

Did you find at least three areas where you might need to change? Most of us could benefit by altering a few of our attitudes.

PART
TWO

The Big Eight

This past summer my daughter Mary and I worked at the Nebraska State Fair in a booth designed to raise money for third-world workers. Among the items we sold was a long tube that made a beautiful sound when tilted.

Hawking our wares, we called this the "rainmaker." Since the Midwest had suffered a lot of flooding that year, most people were repelled when we tried to sell them a "rainmaker." After a few frustrating hours of no sales for that item, we changed our tune and called it a "rain stopper." Only then did we get some of the curious to actually touch the thing and ask questions.

Smart people learn what to say and what to swallow. We've asked many teens to tell us what adult phrases turn them off. They gave us over thirty conversation killers. From those we narrowed the list to eight big stranglers:

1. "When I was your age . . ."
2. "You just don't understand!"
3. "You only think you have problems."

4. "I don't have time to listen now."
5. "Do what I say, not what I do."
6. "Because I told you to!"
7. "Why can't you be more like . . ."
8. "You'll look back someday . . ."

Each of these statements says more to the teen-ager than the statement itself. Instead of hearing your actual words, your teen hears you saying

1. Your problems aren't important because I had it much tougher when I was your age.

2. You aren't capable of understanding, so there is no sense in explaining it.

3. Teenagers only have mini-problems.

4. I am too busy to be pestered by a teenager's little world.

5. You do what's right; I don't have to.

6. I don't want to bother with your attempts to negotiate.

7. I wish you were someone else.

8. Forget about today and concentrate on to-morrow.

Whether you use any of the above statements is not the ultimate question. Look beneath the surface of what you do say to your teen. Do you put across a negative, destructive meaning?

Practice saying "Do it any way you want" with various inflections. The words aren't as important as the meaning behind them. This statement can mean several things, depending on the way it is said:

You are free to do as you please.

You can do as you stubbornly please.

You better not dare do that.

Later the parent may claim, "Well, I told him he could do it, didn't I?" when, in fact, he implied by his tone of voice that he had better not do it.

Think about what you say, especially the things you say over and over again. Your vocabulary and/ or tone of voice might be a huge red light in your relationship with your teenager.

7

"When I Was Your Age . . ."

Would you like to drive a healthy teen totally out of his mind? Would you like to hear his teeth grind, watch his eyes roll into the back of his head, and see his brain smoke? All parents have to do is say, "When I was your age . . ."

It would be hard to find a worse way to start a sentence. Teens all over the world climb the walls every time they hear the phrase.

A young person once said to me that he was getting ready for the day when he would tell his children those wonderful "When I was your age . . ." tales. He said he would tell his kids, "Why, when I was your age I had to get up out of the chair and walk all the way across the room just to change channels."

Now who's going to believe that story?

Why Does It Grind?

The problem isn't the old stories. As we have suggested in our chapter on storytelling, stories can be valuable and appreciated. To many teens the phrase "When I was your age . . ." suggests a deep and serious rift between parent and young person. It sends up these red flags:

1. The parent isn't listening.
2. The teen has most likely heard this story many times.
3. The parent lives in the past and can't get up to speed.
4. The parent may still feel sorry for himself.
5. The parent can't understand the current problems that confront teens.
6. This phrase often means the parent is about to oversimplify the problem.

Teenagers are intelligent and reason with computer-like speed. By the time the parent begins the sentence, the young person is thinking that at least four of the six things listed above are true.

Parents are capable of understanding their teens. We can learn about today's culture and its current problems. Many do. Unfortunately, the phrase "When I was your age . . ." sounds like we are not attempting to bridge that gap.

It's a Standoff

Notice what happens:

The teen says to his or her parent, "My teacher keeps putting me down in class. . . ." And the parent replies, "You think you've got a problem? Let me tell you what I used to deal with. . . ."

They just passed each other on the highway.

The teen was driving a remodeled sports car. The parent was driving a Crown Victoria. And they were heading in different directions.

Alternatives

Instead of leading off with a statement that says "I only understand the past and I don't have time for you," look for ways that are more likely to gain instant rapport. Something like:

"I didn't find it easy to be a teen either. Tell me what's going on with you."

The speaker empathizes with the teen and keeps the spotlight on the young person. Otherwise it's a debate over who had the worst time.

Another good opener might be:

"It must be tough to be a teen in today's world. What's the hard part for you?"

This statement is not self-centered or misdirected. The speaker knows everyone hurts and is open to hear what kind of pain this teen is experiencing.

Try, "Some days are great and other days are the pits. What have your days been like lately?"

This exchange is a step above "Yep, ain't it awful?" by acknowledging the fact that life has an upside as well as a downside. This allows the teen the opportunity to choose the direction of the conversation. The parent has just provided the fork in the road. If every adult statement is negative, the teen is more likely to take a negative tack too.

The real goal here is to improve communication with our teens. And one way to get better at this is to ask ourselves if our statements open up conversation and encourage it or close it down. Do we build walls or open pathways?

Sounds Like Sour Grapes

The words "When I was your age . . ." are almost never followed by a positive statement. What the teen is about to hear is how tough the parent used to have it and how totally grateful every young person should be.

"Sour grapes" is a term that pops up a couple of times in the Bible. "The fathers have eaten sour grapes, and the children's teeth are set on edge" (Jeremiah 31:29b; see also Ezekiel 18:2).

If fathers and mothers are bitter about their childhood, it is of little benefit to share those memories with their children. Especially if the purpose of telling the stories is to make the young person feel guilty because they have it so good.

Instead of speaking about the hardship and sacrifice of our past, we might put more emphasis on the good times. Compare the sour grapes passage with the stories the psalmist told about happiness and God's generosity.

"I will utter things hidden from of old—things we have heard and known, things our fathers have told us. We will not hide them from their children; we will tell the next generation the praiseworthy deeds of the Lord, his power, and the wonders he has done" (Psalm 78:2b–4).

Teens would far rather hear about God's blessing on your life than to hear how many holes were in your shoes. They would rather know about your hikes in the Rockies than to hear how far you carried a milk pail. They want to hear about the times your family laughed around the table rather than how stern old Grandpa was.

If we don't talk about the good times, our teenagers will think we had none.

8

"You Just Don't Understand!"

Your frustrated teen stands at the front door ready to leave for the evening. You have been arguing about money, curfews, cars, boyfriends, clothing, grades, chores, etc. . . . With the dispute unresolved and hanging over her head, the young person shrugs her shoulders and departs very unhappily, mumbling, "You just don't understand."

Amazingly, parents often share the same feeling. Unable to convince their teen that her behavior is risky, Mom or Dad finally bellow out that primitive theme, "You just don't understand!"

What does this tell us? Both parent and teen share the identical frustrations. Neither believes the other is able to understand what he or she is saying, facing, or feeling.

Picture a great chasm with a parent standing on one side and a teen standing on the other. A swinging wooden bridge stretches between the two sides, but neither person is willing to cross to the other side.

If that's the case (and it often is), parents need to find a way to cross to the other side. The only way to do that is to reach out and understand how the other feels and deals with life.

What Do Parents Understand?

There are certain things about teens that we understand, simply because our experience gives us insight.

These are some things most parents understand:

- what hunger does to a person
- how lack of sleep affects people
- what temptation can lead to
- how today's decisions affect tomorrow
- what regrets are
- how fleeting the teen years are
- being deprived of something doesn't mean we will "just die"
- only God lasts forever
- bad company can leave scars
- even rebellion must be tempered
- authority is necessary
- sex is not synonymous with love
- the difference between being used and being accepted
- an abusive situation shouldn't be tolerated
- dares are for dopes
- idealism is only half good
- God can help the human spirit snap back
- it's okay to cry yourself to sleep sometimes
- responsibility builds character

These are basically experience-centered truths. We learned them by going through many situations and by watching others go through them. They fall into the category of wisdom.

Unfortunately most teenagers aren't in the market for what we have to sell. Wisdom sounds dull, unimaginative, and restrictive. And they aren't clamoring for someone to tell them about boundaries.

What Teens Understand

I took the question of understanding to teenagers and asked them to explain it. What is it that they know about being a teen that adults might fail to understand?

1. *Teens are victims of stereotyping.* Adults read the newspapers and watch television and believe they understand teens. From that expanse they conclude that teens are boozing, drugging, sexing, and cruising. These might be far from the facts, or at least only superficial actions. The *only* way to know a teen is to talk to one.

2. *Teens seek freedom.* Freedom is a young person's goal. They believe an adult goal is to make a teen comply and become dull like their parents.

3. *They don't like being compared.* A teen is like no other teen. They resent being compared, whether it's favorably or unfavorably. Young people want to stand on their own two feet and represent themselves.

4. *Teens want to make their own choices.* The height of respect is to let a human being make decisions. If they can't choose (to a large extent) their own clothing and music, they feel like children. As they see it, too many parents are afraid to let a

teen make decisions and live with the consequences.

5. *There is disdain for their culture.* When teens leave the house they spend all day in a teen village. There are risks in their village and there is fulfillment in their village. When adults act like the village culture is stupid or insignificant, they denounce what is highly important to the teen. This leads to war.

We ask for compliance to the adult culture while we reject their culture. Teens fear that a parent's goal is to eradicate the youth culture.

Teens ask parents to cut them some slack and try not to oppose everything just because a young person suggests it. Haircuts, clothing, and games may not be wrong, they just may be different.

What Adults and Teens Do Well

Adults. When it comes to the long range, parents understand a great deal. They have experience and wisdom. They know that actions have consequences. Parents need to be respected for what they understand.

Teens. They tend to understand "now" very well. "Now" is important. Teens don't want to sacrifice the present for something promised tomorrow.

The catch is for each age group to compromise. Each must learn respect for the other and make adjustments. When either group is unwilling to do that, friction is inevitably the result.

A Biblical Perspective

The failure of parents and teens to understand and appreciate each other is an ancient puzzle.

This is not the first generation in which parents have struggled against teens, each bewildered by how the other thinks.

Fortunately the Bible gives us dependable guidelines about how understanding affects us and what to do about it. Every concerned human being must try to bridge this gap and attempt to understand those around them.

1. *We all cry to be understood.* This isn't peculiar to any age group or any time. Parents and teens share the same feelings of frustration. We feel that our hopes, fears, and dreams are not being heard.

The apostle Paul tells us he is understood only in part. He hopes to be understood fully (2 Corinthians 1:13–14). The author of Proverbs (2:3) tells his son to cry out for understanding.

2. *Understanding is not exclusive to adults.* Too many parents believe teens cannot understand life, either as a whole or its components. Teens think adults can't imagine what it's like to be young. Understanding is not the exclusive property of any age group.

"It is not only the old who are wise, not only the aged who understand what is right" (Job 32:9).

3. *Too many of us listen without trying to understand.* When someone explains his situation, we may be too busy trying to think of our next comeback.

Careful, caring attention will lead to better insight. Superficial listening only makes the distance greater.

"Be ever hearing, but never understanding; be ever seeing, but never perceiving" (Isaiah 6:9).

4. *Our understanding is faulty.* A "know-it-all" attitude is disastrous. Our perceptions are

flawed and biased. We need the grace of God to help us understand people who are different than ourselves.

"Lean not on your own understanding" (Proverbs 3:5).

5. *If we pay attention, we can gain understanding.* Our impatience and our arrogance tell us we already know everything. We need to hear each other out and try to put ourselves in the other person's situation.

"Pay attention and gain understanding" (Proverbs 4:1).

6. *We can learn to appreciate each other.* Anyone who succeeds in understanding a teen will be accepted by that youth. Teens think no one tries to see life from their perspective. If an adult makes a good effort, he will find favor in the eyes of that youth.

"Good understanding wins favor" (Proverbs 13:15).

7. *People who understand speak more wisely.* Have you ever interrupted someone mid-sentence in order to say something inappropriate? By taking the time to truly listen, we will say fewer things we later regret. First find out what really is going on, and then speak.

"But a man of understanding holds his tongue" (Proverbs 11:12).

8. *God gives understanding.* We can ask God to calm us down, make us loving, and give us insight into what makes our teen tick. A prayer of humility is the invitation for the Holy Spirit to give guidance.

Most Teens Mean No Harm

Generally speaking, teens have no interest in hurting their parents or in hurting themselves.

Even though their search for identity, independence, and individuality often runs against their parents' grain, it usually isn't malicious behavior. Misguided, maybe? Overreacting, probably? Bewildering, definitely. But almost never intentionally mean.

Take the time to read 1 Samuel 24:1–13 and look at young David's frustration. King Saul believes David is trying to kill him. That isn't what David wants at all. The former shepherd sneaks in and cuts off a corner of Saul's robe while the king is asleep. Certainly if he had wanted to kill him he could have. Saul fears David and refuses to trust him.

Listen to David's plea. He is an earnest young man desperate to be understood. (He calls Saul "father" when in reality he is his father-in-law.)

"See, my father, look at this piece of your robe in my hand! I cut off the corner of your robe but did not kill you. Now understand and recognize that I am not guilty of wrongdoing or rebellion. I have not wronged you, but you are hunting me down to take my life" (v. 11).

We think teens are involved in a gigantic plot to drive adults out of their minds. Consequently, the response is often to want to stomp on them for fear they will take over the land.

Teens may do things that are wrong. Teens need to be corrected when they do, and most need a good dose of discipline, but most of all teens need to be taken seriously and understood.

9

"You Only *Think* You Have Problems"

Few adults ever tell us they wish they could go back to become teenagers again. While we have many good memories, those years also represent a great deal of hurt, loss, pain, and disappointment. The goal of high school was to graduate and become free. Most of us were extremely relieved when that finally happened.

As parents we collect our own set of agonies. Job stress, bills, ill-health, marital tension, and other calamities overtake us and soon we forget what kind of pain teenagers face. We are tempted to minimize teenagers' problems. To us, adult troubles are real and teen troubles are small, insignificant, "puppy" problems.

In truth young people have a multitude of losses. Those losses are real, deep, and often affect them for a lifetime. If we are to understand our teenagers, we need to look beneath the surface and find out what it is tumbling in on them.

I have asked teenagers to describe their hurts. Some of their problems surprised me. Without any order of importance, let's look at the pain as they have described it.

Death

Teenagers are likely to have been to the funeral of a grandparent or two. While it is a sad experience for many, it is not usually devastating. In many cases they have seen the death coming or have been told that the grandparent was likely to die. That gave them time to adjust and begin the grief process gradually.

A deeper problem is a teenager's bewilderment at this time. If they aren't close to their grandparent or live far away, they don't know how they are "supposed" to feel. In truth they are attending the funeral of a near stranger. They feel guilty because their heart isn't broken. Some even wish that were the case; it may be easier to deal with.

Teenagers hear stories or see pictures of grandparents taking their grandchildren fishing or on other outings, but that may not have been true in their situation. They are likely to mourn the lack of relationship as much as the death.

It would be helpful if parents would ask them how they are feeling, rather than assume that they are grief stricken.

Many teenagers also face the death of a friend. When a teenager dies, whether by illness, accident, or suicide, he or she affects a wide circle of students. Teenagers are stunned and hurt.

A teenager in a small town was killed in an auto/train accident. The next day there was only an eerie silence at school. The administration and teachers felt it best not to discuss the youth's death. Thankfully, this has changed in most schools, and counselors are made available.

Young people would very much like to talk about the death of a friend. Their own emotions are deep and complicated. They are shaken not only by the event but also by their own sense of mortality. Schools, churches, and parents can help minister to a teen's needs when these tragedies occur.

Loss of Friendships

One teenage girl volunteered that all of her friends seemed to move away. When this happens a young person's trust factor is often damaged. Some adults feel that these cannot be significant relationships, but they often are. After a close friend moves away, it is hard at first to develop a similar friendship. A teen doesn't want to be hurt again. When it happens too often, they may retreat and steer clear of any close involvement with others.

Equally difficult for a teen is to have a friend drop them. This is fairly common. Either one of the two intentionally ends the relationship, or one of them simply drifts away and finds other friends.

"We were real close for a while," a sophomore boy told me of a friendship. "Then he got involved in sports. He plays varsity in practically everything and it's like we're in two different worlds. I still like him and all, but it doesn't seem to work out to be close friends anymore."

There are movements from social strata to social strata. Suddenly a young person becomes serious about getting a scholarship and joins a couple of academic clubs. Another teen joins the party crowd and drifts away from his old friends. Those shifts are serious disappointments to the person who has been left behind.

In the long run the teenager learns to cope with the instability of friendships, but it is a painful process. Even short-term summer camp friendships are hard to end. When relationships are terminated, the loss is extremely real to the youth who is involved.

Rejection

The school cafeteria often determines the ins and outs of social acceptance. Imagine eight students who normally sit at a particular table. Sometimes there are six and other times ten. The basic core who sit there usually have something in common. It could be sports or academics or church or cars or mischief or cheerleading or student government, but something holds their interest and gives them common ground.

If someone from another segment of the school tries to sit there, he or she is normally rejected. The rejection might be anything from a cool reception to an angry "Get out of here." Either way, the person certainly knows that he or she is not welcome there.

Similar barriers exist throughout life. But it seems to be more difficult to handle through the teenage years. Few of us are good at being loners because we were created to have contact with other people.

The teen world is the place where teens first meet with serious rejection by their peers. They begin to recognize an invisible caste system and they stumble trying to learn how to deal with it.

Many teenagers feel a greater sense of rejection when they start to date. The poor and the rich, the bright and the slow—all experience some trouble relating to each other on this basis, and will run in to some obstacles.

Those who hold on to the dream of equality find that dream rudely shattered. Society has its glass walls and glass ceilings. Most young people have trouble breaking out of their limits. It is usually a shock to learn that the whole world is not their oyster; life is not a bowl of cherries, and you can't necessarily be anything you want to be.

This is not a new phenomenon. The author of Ecclesiastes sees young people as anxious, troubled, and empty (11:10). It has typically been a vexing time of uneasy changes.

They Lose Their Invincibility

You don't have to be a social scientist to know that young people tend to feel invincible. They think they can do anything and come out on top. Teenagers take risks, dream, explore, taste, and try life. It would appear that they are over-confident and even arrogant.

There is considerable truth to this, but there is also a painful side to the issue. During their teen years young people learn that there are chinks in their armor. They find out that they are not likely to become the homecoming queen or football quarterback. And though their parents love them dearly, they are not king of the hill.

All of us have to learn this in life, and it is never easy. Teenagers are regularly faced with the facts—

they may not be fast, tall, good-looking, have big biceps, or a small waist.

Like an onion, layer after layer is removed. Soon they are brought down to a size they didn't expect.

It is a genuine sense of loss. But many maintain the feeling that nothing can destroy them. That's why they take chances—like driving too fast, drinking too much, experimenting with drugs, or having premarital sex. Many still practice unsafe sex, convinced that nothing will happen to them. Though they may feel indestructible, they no longer see themselves as perfect. To the contrary, they now concentrate on their imperfections.

I can remember what must have been my most humiliating day as a youth. Like most boys, I picked on girls in a desperate attempt to get their attention. On this occasion I tiptoed up behind a female and knocked her books out of her hands and quickly ran away. As I dashed down the street I heard footsteps behind me. Who in the world would be chasing me? Looking over my shoulder I saw that same girl hot on my heels. And she was gaining.

Dumbfounded, I poured on the speed and looked back again, fully expecting to see her fading figure. But, no! She was still on my trail and her figure kept getting larger. I could hear her heavy breathing like a hound dog in pursuit of a coon. Darting to the left and then the right like a Dallas Cowboy I-back, I then felt her long-fingered hand grab my shoulder. As she pulled me backward with one hand, she began pummeling me over the head with her purse.

How could it happen? In my worst nightmare I never imagined that a female would chase me or could catch me, let alone beat me over the head. But this shameless girl did it and destroyed part of my confidence forever. To this day, the thought of knocking something out of a girl's hand and running causes me to shudder.

Breaking Up With a Girlfriend/Boyfriend

How much loss is suffered from breaking up depends on the extent of involvement—how long a period they had been dating, how high were the expectations of each, how close they were to a big event, whether or not they had exchanged rings or given another sign of commitment. Had they reached an understanding of where this relationship might lead? Were they sexually active? Did she get dropped in favor of another person? Did he get dumped or was he the dumper?

Parents are unwise to treat teenage breakups as "puppy love." While they are young and the relationship may have been short, the pain and loss are still very real to the teen. They may need someone to talk to, and that person could be a parent. Be willing to spend long hours, especially late at night. If your teen chooses to talk to you at this time, consider it a great opportunity to bond and help.

Often teens want to know if their parents broke up with each other or with others when they were young and how they felt. They also want to know what it feels like to be in love and how you know for sure. If those moments present themselves, never brush them off.

Siblings Moving Out

It may have been the day they lived to see, but now that it has arrived, they're sad. Siblings aren't exactly heroes of each other but they usually are at least friends. When one leaves, more space is created in the family, but their absence also makes a hole that no one else will ever be able to fill.

Don't be surprised if teenagers mope around for a while after a brother or sister leaves home. They will soon adjust. It helps a lot if they can look forward to a visit.

An adult told me that when he was a teenager his parents trivialized everything that was important to him:

Girlfriends were "puppy love."

Cars were considered a waste of money.

Sports were frivolous.

Friends were disregarded.

Social events were ridiculed.

Clothes were laughed at.

His music choice was called sinful.

Not one part of his life was given meaning by his parents. It was as if he would not become a person until he passed his twenty-first birthday.

The losses experienced by today's teenagers are not much different than they were a generation ago. Personal losses are significant and that fact doesn't change. The problem is that many adults are prone to forget what teen pain was like. Maybe that's good for our own survival. But for the sake of our young people we need to listen, remember, and try to understand so we can be open to help during the times when they face a world of hurt.

10

"I Don't Have Time to Listen Now"

"I can't get my teenager to talk," a mother told me in frustration. "I've tried everything. It seems like the more I talk, the less she talks. I've even tried sitting with her and saying nothing, but that doesn't work either. I'm at my wit's end."

If parents of teens had a song, the previous paragraph would be the chorus. Commonly teens clam up and refuse to get into a conversation with adults who are in authority. That's particularly true if that authority happens to be a parent.

The straightforward fact is that we might never "get our teen to talk" very much. The important question is how do we create an atmosphere where a teen might feel comfortable talking? A teen might refuse to talk under the best of conditions, but a parent's task is not to make the teen talk as much as it is to remove obstacles.

One of the best things we can do is to create a

healthy habit of listening. If the teen believes his parent has good ears, he is far more likely to speak his mind.

A Good Listener

I keep getting advertising notices inviting me to come in and see if I need a hearing aid. I don't know who submitted my name, but the fact is I have a far worse hearing problem than a hearing aid will solve: I hear words but I don't always hear what the person means. I don't always hear how they feel, or what they want. I don't hear where they are going with what they are saying.

And I'm afraid they haven't invented a hearing aid that will cure my problem.

The difficulty isn't new. You will remember that Jesus ran into people with a similar ailment. When He made the plea "He who has ears to hear, let him hear" (Luke 8:8), Jesus was calling for spiritual listening. In order to hear teens we need to shift to another level of listening. Our mind, our soul, and our heart must listen too.

When adults believe that teen-talk is superficial and unimportant, they do not listen well. They only process the words without looking for their meaning.

If we are unable to hear the teen, we are unable to help. One of the biggest mistakes we make is to answer a young person before we have heard him or her. Proverbs said it before we did: "He who answers before listening—that is his folly and his shame" (18:13).

Good ears listen. Good ears hear more than the waves on the surface. There are many sounds beneath the sea that we never hear (but they are there).

The Need for a Listening Ear Is a Spiritual Need

One of the basic spiritual needs of individuals is the longing for someone to listen. Teens feel that acutely. They don't lack for people who are eager to tell them something. Advisors line up everywhere. The shortage is of people who want to hear what teens have to say.

Recently I attended a seminar on parenting. The speaker, a leading psychologist, lamented the loss of the good old days when children were seen and not heard. "Children shouldn't talk," he said; they don't have anything to say anyway.

I didn't stay for the afternoon session.

There is a fundamental misunderstanding of youth in his statement. Young people have a great deal that is worth saying. The very fact that they need to say it makes it valuable. They shouldn't be allowed to interrupt others, but their observations, evaluations, insights, and emotions that go with it are extremely important.

I hold seminars for teachers. In one of our sessions we ask the participants to write down the marks of a good teacher. Invariably the number one or number two characteristic of a good teacher is that the person is a good listener. Not a good talker but a good listener.

Likewise, a good parent is one who takes the time to listen.

One of God's major activities is listening to His children. Listening is a spiritual encounter.

What Is Listening?

The American philosopher Mortimer Adler says we get into trouble because we believe that listening is a passive activity. In order to become a better listener, we have to see it as an active encounter.

Active listening is hard work. It even requires a new way of treating people. If we aren't used to it we will need to practice this approach. Let's look at five types of listening. The next time your teen starts to talk, ask yourself which of the five levels you are on. Then, decide if you need to move to another type. This kind of awareness will begin to sharpen your skills.

1. *Vacant listening.* This means the teen is talking but you're out to lunch. You know words are coming your way, but you don't care what he or she says.

In your mind you are shuffling through your recipe box, worrying about the phone bill, or planning your work list for tomorrow. Secretly you hope this won't take long because you want to go jogging.

Vacant listening is one of the most common forms. If people ask you how you are today, they almost never listen for the answer. Next time answer, "Oh, my mother's in jail on racketeering charges," and see if the person even flinches.

Most of us know we are surrounded by vacant listening. When we say no one listens to us, often that is exactly correct.

Say to yourself, "My teen is talking; am I here or has my brain left for the beach?"

2. *Defensive listening.* Adam comes into the room and says, "I need to borrow the car Thursday

night." He goes on to explain why he wants the vehicle. Essentially Adam is wasting his breath, because his mother is already searching for a reason why the car will be unavailable.

That's defensive listening.

The parent has shifted immediately from the teen's need to use the car to her own strong instinct to preserve the vehicle. No effective listening is going on because said parent is looking for a way to protect herself rather than a way to understand and help her son.

"The car needs new brakes," she blurts.

"But I was going to use it Thursday night."

"I haven't paid up the insurance," she stalls.

Basically this is an example of a harried attempt to rescue what is ours from the hands of a teenager. There is nothing wrong with self-preservation. It's even healthy. But too often we let our defenses block our ears and shut out what the teen is saying.

Defensive listening is self-centered listening. It stops us from making spiritual contact with the speaker.

3. *Active listening.* Don't you love talking to someone who hangs on your every word? Her face lights up. She asks just enough questions to keep the conversation going. She acts like she wants to hear more. If something isn't clear she asks for more information.

It's fun to talk to an active listener. The next time you need someone to hear you out, you will go back to the same person. Teens do the same thing.

Active listening is an art that can be cultivated. The listener must practice skills like

- concentration
- caring
- measured responses
- encouraging questions
- a sense of togetherness.

If we are in the habit of passive listening, it takes work to cross over and become an active listener. But the effort promises to pay big dividends.

4. *Perceptive listening.* If someone tells us life is tough right now for them, we don't stop to analyze what they mean by that. If we do, we may miss what they say next about what they are going through.

How do you feel if your teen uses a vulgar word? Are you shocked, embarrassed, angry, horrified? If that's all you are, you've missed the message. A perceptive listener wonders why the teen used the word. Was it out of frustration? Was it merely to shock you? Was it a sign of desperation? Was it a plea for help? Was it a call for more attention? Or was it simply carelessness?

A perceptive listener pays attention to the

- tone of voice
- sense of urgency
- facial expression
- body language
- circumstance surrounding the outburst or speech.

The entire person communicates. Words are limited in their ability to deliver a message.

What does a teenager mean, for example, when he says, "I hate living here"? For one thing he might mean exactly that, he hates living here. But too many parents panic at such words. Smart parents will keep their cool and look for the underlying message. *Why* does he hate living here? Is there something unreasonable about living here? What is he going through right now? Is he experiencing some difficulty that he isn't telling you about?

Look for the worm in the core. Don't spend all of your time trying to polish the apple.

5. *Sensitive listening.* Sensitive listening is "putting yourself into someone else's shoes."

This is the ultimate in listening. Putting yourself in another person's shoes doesn't mean you have to agree with him or her. Sensitive listening means you try to feel what that person feels. That person might be wrong. He or she may need a definitive no for an answer. But the listener who is sensitive will at least make an attempt to hear what the teen is feeling and put himself in his or her place.

Imagine that all your daughter's friends are going to a party at the river. There will be almost as much alcohol as there is water, you are sure. She promises not to drink but she believes she desperately needs to go to the party.

Can you feel what she feels? Can you feel the loneliness? Can you feel the sense of separation? Can you feel the need to be accepted? Can you feel the drive to have fun with her peers?

Only then can you hear what she just said. And if you can't feel it, you live in another world and the distance between the two of you is a chasm.

If you tell her she can't go, be sure you heard what she asked and that you feel her sense of loss. You may need to refuse her, you do need to protect her, but remember that she may be terribly hurt in the process.

The next time a young person begins to talk to

you, mentally run down the list. While he is speaking, are you

1. Vacant?
2. Defensive?
3. Active?
4. Perceptive?
5. Sensitive?

A good listener will not be guilty of numbers one and two and will seek to become numbers three, four, and five together. Smart parents hone their listening skills. By improving these skills we will begin to understand our teens better.

11

"Do What I Say, Not What I Do"

I asked a group of teens what they felt was the purpose of life—heavy stuff for any age group. Amazingly this group had no trouble with the question. They agreed that the basic purpose of life was to make money.

When the writer Ernest Hemingway killed himself, he reportedly left a note saying, "Life is a cruel joke." Many teens come to the conclusion that there is no purpose to life, or at least they have an extremely twisted concept of it. When it comes to teen violence, some say that young people have no hope, no meaning in their lives, no direction, no purpose.

Christians know what a life of fulfillment is if they are truly following Christ, and certainly they want to point their children in the direction of fulfillment in Christ. But sometimes parents make lousy pointers. It is futile to tell a teen what to do if in fact you don't do it. You can't have high expectations for your teens while having low expectations for yourself. Teens resent it when adults point them in a direction that they do not follow themselves.

Parents are in an excellent position to communicate purpose to their teens. We have a handle on what life is all about. Maybe we can't fill in all the details, but hopefully we have a grasp on life's real goal:

The goal is spiritual and not physical.

The goal is satisfying but not selfish.

The goal is personal but not private.

The goal is loving but not lustful.

The goal is serving but not demeaning.

One of the major problems with people of all ages is that we spend too much time inspecting our own belly buttons. We are focused on the questions of who we are, where we are going, and how we will please ourselves. In general, we become lost in obsessive self-centeredness and lack any purpose outside of ourselves.

On a recent trip I met a woman who told me she couldn't stand to be around her son. She said that no matter how their conversations began they invariably ended up centered on him.

All of us have met teenagers who are trapped inside of themselves. Too many of us as parents have contributed to this fixation because we have made them the center of our universe. When a parent ends every sentence with "But how will this affect Mark?" Mark just might get the impression that he is the most important thing around here.

The question is twofold:

1. How do we teach a teen the real purpose of life?

2. How do we get that teen to stop staring at himself in the mirror?

To answer the first question is to resolve the second.

What Is Our Purpose?

In case any of us has forgotten why we are here, let's brush up on Christianity 101.

"Love the Lord your God with all your heart and with all your soul and with all your mind and with all your strength. The second is this: Love your neighbor as yourself. There is no commandment greater than these" (Mark 12:30–31).

If this seems an over-simplification to anyone, it is still the foundation to human purpose. Those who totally ignore the words of Christ are highly likely to miss the whole point of life.

The scriptures that teach these principles are many. Only those who lose their life for the sake of the gospel will gain it. The formula runs like this:

Loving God completely, plus loving people who need you, will equal a satisfying sense of purpose.

And we thought life was complicated! Well, it can be. But these guidelines allow life to make genuine sense.

That was the easy part: identifying the purpose of life. The hard part is getting this across to our teens. But be encouraged. Many young people already understand it well. They reach toward the goal with great enthusiasm and dedication. Sometimes they do it better than adults.

Teens Look for Purpose

Last Sunday morning I watched a teenage boy seek out an elderly lady in church. The woman had been sick for some time. A tall youth, he bent down and hugged her. Then he asked with real compassion, "How have you been getting along?"

That young man was a million miles from mugging, threatening, or harassing her. Instead, he reached out to care about someone who lived on an entirely different plane than himself.

Teens may be self-centered, but not all the time. Frequently they want to live a life beyond themselves.

When I was a junior-high student, my main goal was to raise havoc with the system. A wild, disoriented youth, my waking hours were dedicated to creating chaos. Most of my stories would be too gruesome to tell here. (Today, however, they would sound mild in the streets of Washington D.C., where I grew up.)

In the few hours each week when I did something constructive, I helped the poor (though I was poor myself). As an early teen I raised money and collected food to deliver to the needy.

Looking back, it seems I had an almost desperate drive to live outside of myself. "Myself" was too confusing, too tumultuous, too frantic to really enjoy. But for short periods of time I could do some things that were above and beyond me.

I wasn't a Christian at the time. I was certainly far away from hearing the Scriptures. However, even on a purely human level I had a strong urge to discover purpose.

One of the better counseling tools adults can use with teens is to invite them to step outside of themselves and become involved with others. This isn't the only counseling tool. Teens have problems that need to be addressed. They especially resent people who tell them to merely forget their troubles and go do something else.

The invitation to step out of themselves is the call to freedom. They are land-locked and cannot hope to sail. Point the way so they can enjoy some time on the open seas.

How often do we see Christian youth groups encouraging teens to step out of themselves? The group that goes to Appalachia to run Vacation Bible Schools for the summer has the opportunity to reach out instead of reaching in. Those who work in soup kitchens break free from their own turmoil, at least for a while. Teens often respond to the challenge.

What we frequently see are youth groups that major on spiritual introspection. Their primary theme is "What's wrong with you?" and "How can we change that?" That has value, but it is limited. Teens need to spend some time concerned about someone else.

When I see teens running a car wash to raise money for a trip to Florida, I always flinch. My question is "When will they raise money to drill wells in Haiti?" Teens need to know that the purpose of life goes beyond a ride down Thunder Mountain at Bulah Park (though that ride is a lot of fun).

Teens who are asked to donate clothing, food, and cash to a good cause usually respond in a big way. Instinctively they want that kind of purpose and challenge.

How Can Mom and Dad Help?

The number one reason why teens hold on to their Christian faith is because they see an adult living the Christian life. (Read that again.) It is not because they have been taught correctly. It is not because they made a commitment or a pledge. Rather, an adult has made a lasting impression on their very soul.

Since that's true in many instances, how then are teens going to learn the purpose of life? They must see it in the lives of Mom and Dad or some other significant adult.

Last Sunday's lesson on finding meaning in life has little impact unless teens see an adult live out that meaning. In a Christian home Mom and Dad are their best hope.

According to the passage we quoted earlier, our purpose is two-fold: one, to love God; and two, to love our neighbor.

Those are the attributes teens need to see in their parents if they are expected to learn how to live with purpose.

We demonstrate that we love God by our behavior and attitudes. Words are important, but they need to be followed by action. The fruit of the Spirit should be evident in our lives—love, joy, peace, patience, kindness, goodness, faithfulness, gentleness, and self-control (Galatians 5:22). Parents who are grouchy, impatient, mean-spirited, harsh, hateful, and uncaring leave the teen bewildered and confused.

There are other ways to show that we love God, but these nine fruits are the basics. It won't cut it to say what we've done to help build a huge church, or something of that nature, if we can't show love and kindness to our teenager.

The same is true of loving our neighbor. How do you show active love toward others? How do you let others know that you care? Teens that have seen their parents help others have a great heritage.

I have a friend who often takes strangers into his home to stay. He will help the person get a car and a job, even giving him or her a few extra bucks to help out. That is the pattern of this individual's life. He takes risks to get involved in the lives of others. But he has been a great example to his children and now to his grandchildren.

Teenagers should be able to say with the psalmist: "For you have heard my vows, O God; you have given me the heritage of those who fear your name" (61:5).

Everyone deserves a good heritage. Hopefully the one you leave your teenagers will point toward the purpose and meaning found in Jesus Christ.

12

"Because I Told You To!"

Don't you miss the days when one quick answer was all your child expected?

When your nine-year-old asked why Eskimos live in igloos, you said something like, "Because they like them" or, "It keeps their beverages cold." Your answer was curt, to the point, and loaded with authority.

When your young daughter was told to go to bed early and she wanted to know why, you answered, "Because you have a lot to do tomorrow." She shrugged her shoulders and off she went.

Life was simpler when your children were younger and seemed satisfied with a direct, uncomplicated answer to their question. Children have a sense that their parents know more than they do, and they are willing to accept a simple explanation. The fact that Mom or Dad "knows" gives them a sense of security, and they are eager to believe their parents are right.

But—at the onset of a child's puberty parents can kiss the simple life goodbye. By some magical force the adolescent mind kicks into gear and the thought processes will never be so uncomplicated again. From this day on most teens (not all) will challenge every word that tumbles out of their parents' mouths.

Too Harried to Explain

Every parent of a teenager knows the feeling. You get tired of arguing and hassling. You wonder why you can't simply give an order and see the kid obey, just like in the military.

As one parent put it, "You can bet I never asked my parents 'Why?' And I didn't give a lot of excuses, either. If they told me to get a job done, I knew I had better do it. But with teens today you practically have to bribe them to get anything done."

"Just once," said another frustrated parent, "just once couldn't I say 'Do the dishes' and my kid would get up and head for the dishwasher?"

"I don't have time for all of this haggling. If I tell Spencer to shovel the walk, he says, 'Well, it's just going to snow again,' or, 'If we wait it will all melt anyway,' " another parent offered.

It is difficult to debate with our teen every time we want the trash taken out. Many parents merely give up and take it out themselves rather than argue about every task.

Ideally, no parent's request should have to be challenged, but teenagers typically need a wide range of space in which to ask questions. They will take every opportunity to debate what has been said or asked of them.

Even the most harried parent should make an effort to allow his or her teenager to test the waters, even to dissent. They have an inherent need to ask why. Teens deserve as much explanation as anyone, and adults owe it to them to spell out the situation whenever possible.

Granted, some things shouldn't require discussion:

Routine jobs. Don't debate over clearing the table when it's their turn or regular job.

Small tasks. Picking up their shoes and clothes from the living room floor is not a debatable chore.

Common courtesies. Being polite and respectful to family members and guests is not an option.

Do give an explanation when you plan to change routine or enforce new family policy:

New expectations. From this day on we are going to change this . . . ; do something different about . . .

Value judgments. If they aren't allowed to attend a concert or other event they deserve to know why.

Removal of privileges. "We will no longer watch a certain program or TV station" needs explanation and discussion.

Enforced excursions. "We are all going to Grandmother's house next weekend" should be open to questions and plea bargaining.

Restricted friendships. "I don't want you hanging around with that kind of person" deserves more information if it is to be obeyed.

Questions of taste. "We don't allow rap in this house" calls for clarification and discussion. A parent's taste should not always be the deciding factor.

New responsibilities. What part of their college fund is their responsibility to raise? Who washes the car, fills the tank, etc.?

Other subjects could obviously be added to this list, but you get the idea. Anything other than simple, repetitive tasks are best discussed with an adolescent. It will be worth your effort. When in doubt, go the extra mile and try to engage teens in the debate process.

The Bible invites us to come and reason together (Isaiah 1:18) because God knows we are capable of rational thinking. Teens are in the midst of improving their reasoning ability. Adults would be unwise to ignore these emerging talents.

New Cognitive Powers

Throughout the teen years, young people experience a rapid increase in

- assimilation of information,
- choice-making or options,
- social and educational experience,
- opportunities for problem-solving, reasoning,
- curiosity, and resulting consequences.

These factors, along with a phenomenal physical growth spurt are what separate them from children. While young children have all these capabilities, they lie dormant for the most part. But a teenager's mobility, accelerated learning, and changing circumstances place them in a far more sophisticated position to reason.

If we tell teens not to think by saying things like, "Because I said so . . ." we retard their growth in reasoning. It's like giving a child four swimming lessons and then saying, "That's it, that's enough."

It simply isn't fair to insinuate that a teen can't think for herself, or that she can't be trusted with information by which she can make her own decisions.

When teens are told they can't ride on top of elevators, they have a right to ask why. They deserve a better answer than "because I said so." They need to be told how dangerous it is, why it is dangerous (it's probably illegal too), and that you as a parent forbid it. Now he or she is being let in on the details that went into the important decision-making process.

Family Government

Families don't function best when they operate as a democracy, and certainly not when governed by a dictatorship. We've established that teens don't want to always be told what to do, but they don't always warrant an equal vote in the family either.

Teens prosper when their abilities to understand and make decisions are respected. Simply dictating what is to be done demonstrates your own impatience, frustration, lack of respect for the teen, and a certain amount of insecurity.

Play it smart. Don't cut your teen off at the knees. Allow plenty of room for the inquiring adolescent mind to breathe.

13

"Why Can't You Be More Like. . . ?"

I had been in junior high school only a couple of days when one of the teachers told me her dream. She hoped I wasn't going to be like my oldest brother, Jim. His trouble-making had left a trail through the local school system and had managed to leave his shadow lingering in the halls.

Her purpose may have been to intimidate me early on, before I got loose. Maybe she was trying to inspire me to higher levels than my famous sibling had attained. Whatever she had in mind, I remember feeling embarrassed and hurt. I also recall pleading in my own heart for the opportunity to be judged on my own merits.

There is something inherently wrong with being compared to someone else, especially in your own family. I think anyone would resent it. No one wants to be told that his sister was the greatest student or that his brother was the worst. It's a tremendous burden to be expected to live up to someone else's accomplishments, or to feel that you have to live down someone else's reputation. Everyone wants to stand on their own two feet and give a full account of themselves.

The apostle Paul warned us against trying to find our identity by comparing ourselves to others. The full measure of a person can only be found within his or her own heart.

"Each one should test his own actions. Then he can take pride in himself, without comparing himself to somebody else, for each one should carry his own load" (Galatians 6:4–5).

Comparisons can be devastating no matter how well intended they may be. Instead of complimenting the person, a comparison more often wounds.

The Desire to Motivate

Parents and teachers of teens are preoccupied with the task of trying to motivate them. How will we get them to shape up, take life seriously, and make something of themselves? Often the harder we try, the less we accomplish. Motivation comes from within, an inspiration from the least expected direction. Overt, direct, heavy-handed attempts at motivation invariably fail.

The parent or teacher means well, to be sure. But in their dedication they sometimes use less than tactful methods. Comparing one teen with another is an approach designed for disaster.

The Real Message

No matter how pure the adult's motives might be, the message the teen gets is "I don't like you the way you are. If you were more like So-and-So I would like you more."

In response to the comparison many teens will think, "I'll never be like So-and-So. I don't even want to be like So-and-So. What's the use in trying?"

There are better measuring rods. Point the teenager to standards like

- What does the youth expect of himself?
- What does his family expect in behavior?
- What does the Lord expect of him as a Christian?
- What does society demand of his conduct?

These are valid expectations; they represent important values. It isn't that no standards exist. The problem comes when a teen is compared to others.

"You like her better, don't you?"

Have you ever heard that challenge? If you have, you may have thought your daughter was *asking* to be compared to her sister. Actually it's a trap. She's laid the bait and there is only one answer she is looking for. She would like to hear that you like her best. It's an adolescent version of "Mirror, mirror on the wall." She wants to know that she is the fairest of them all. No other answer will do.

Smart parents avoid this game. Don't answer the question. Sidestep it and say, "I think you're great. I love being around you." Too many parents grab at the bait. They tend to answer, "Why, honey, I love both of you equally." To which the teen will answer, "Yeah, but she gets better grades than I do." And so the argument will go on.

Make it crystal clear that you accept, love, and enjoy your daughter or son totally on the basis of who he or she is. Your appreciation of a person has nothing to do with how you think of anyone else.

Another good answer to the dreaded claim, "You like her better, don't you?" is, "All I know is how much I like you. I don't make comparisons."

But in order to rise to the occasion, you have to mean it. A teen has a remarkable ability to see through your feelings and can tell when you're faking it. Deal honestly with your feelings and acceptance or non-acceptance of your teenager.

No Favorites

Have you ever asked a parent how her daughter is getting along and seen an immediate smile, twinkle in her eye, rise in her voice? Then, when you asked how her son was doing, her face showed a perceptible drop, her eyes grew dim, and her voice turned grave?

I've seen that response over and over again. I may have even done it myself. One thing is for certain: If you and I can see that transition in a parent's face, so can a teenager! They *know* when we appreciate or approve of one child over another.

Teenagers are great detectives. They pick up clues quickly. That means parents cannot afford to have a favorite child. Our natural tendency is to gravitate toward a child with whom we better relate, or whose personality we favor, and in doing so neglect the other. I propose that this is an ungodly habit. Get hold of yourself, adjust your attitude, and increase your love and affection for the child that you feel less akin to for whatever reason.

Some parents protest that it isn't that easy. Of course it isn't. But that doesn't mean it can't be done. And remember, you can't fake it. It must become a fact, a reality.

Let's take a look at God's example:

"Peter began to speak, 'I now realize how true it is that God does not show favoritism' " (Acts 10:34).

God is our model and inspiration. His Holy Spirit gives us the strength to do what we would humanly find extremely difficult. Begin to think about what you like about each of your teenagers and concentrate on it. Ask yourself what you don't like and learn to bear it or see the good side of it. Look for assets you may have missed. Spend time with your son or daughter even when it is inconvenient or trying.

It isn't only that we can't *say* we have a favorite. We can't afford to *feel* like we have a favorite. Turn your good intentions and posturing into reality.

Practice Thankfulness

There is lots to think about and be concerned about when you have teenagers in your home—the clothes, the cars, the social life, the curfews, the whole ball of wax. But if you want to keep your sanity, work on thankfulness.

What are your teenager's good points? This may take some effort, but you can do it. What is it that others like about her? Maybe her friends see some good qualities that you have ignored or overlooked. Parents who cannot see any good qualities in their teen have gone over the edge and need to reassess their own attitudes.

The apostle Paul said, "I thank my God every time I remember you" (Philippians 1:3).

Parents could help stabilize their situation by

aiming for the same goal where their teens are concerned.

We need God's wisdom and strength to love our teen as He does, and to stop comparing him to others.

14

"You'll Look Back Someday . . ."

It is hard to imagine a less effective threat than "You'll look back someday. . . ." The only person who can relate to this kind of a statement is someone who is looking back.

Usually the comment is built on frustration because no other argument seems to work, and more than likely the parent that says it is implying that he will someday look at his teen and say, "I told you so."

Giving this kind of a warning reveals that the parent is forgetting that teens are wrapped up in today, not tomorrow. And no young person ever expects to have any regrets, so you might as well not talk about it.

A teen with a good sense of humor will hear this and immediately picture his parents thirty years from now—gray-haired, bifocaled, arms folded, brows downcast, lips curled, and possibly a tapping toe. In low, measured tones he hears the parents deliver, "Didn't I tell you you'd look back someday. . . ?"

It's frightfully close to the truth, isn't it?

The Parent Is Right

It's the plain truth that makes this useless prophecy particularly painful. While the teen is collecting memories, he or she is also gathering regrets. But they are unlikely to look into the future. Teens are too busy trying to get themselves through the rapidly changing present. They seldom respond to what their feelings might be like tomorrow.

The Bible is filled with sowing and reaping. Cause and effect are strong themes in the Scriptures.

"As I have observed, those who plow evil and those who sow trouble, reap it" (Job 4:8).

"Cast your bread upon the waters, for after many days you will find it again" (Ecclesiastes 11:1).

From sheer experience parents try to plan for what will happen "many days" later. Teens suffer the "immediate." They don't have a clue how the parties today will affect them five years from now, but they do know how it will affect them this weekend.

Teens don't live hand to mouth like a baby, but they do tend to live weekend to weekend.

With a minimum of retooling we could reshape the age-old phrase and greatly increase its impact. Move the wisdom of the ages, repackage it, and deliver it in terms teens can appreciate this afternoon:

"If you go to that party, you will be grounded and lose the car this weekend."

That they understand. The consequences are immediate.

"If you flunk history you will stay home week-nights until you improve your grades."

They see the cause and effect. The downside is directly related to misbehavior.

The Bible encourages us to sow in order to please the Spirit for eternity (Galatians 6:8). It warns us not to sow sin because we will reap destruction. Those are vital concepts, but teens are less concerned about the benefits of eternity and more focused on today. Make more of a point as to how the Holy Spirit can work through us on a daily, sixty-minute per hour basis.

The Place of Guilt

Guilt does play a proper role in parent/teen relationships. We do mess up and we are to blame for what we do. The problem arises when either parent or teen tries to use guilt as a club to beat the other over the head.

The "Someday..." statement is laden with guilt. It implies that the teen will someday feel terrible because of what he is doing or not doing now. The truth is, maybe he will and maybe he won't.

As parents we need to remember that guilt is not the best motivator. Shame is a lousy way to modify behavior. And sometimes the sense of guilt only serves to make the teen more rebellious. He or she responds by saying, "There's nothing wrong with this," and doubles the energy to prove it.

"Well," a parent insists, "you should feel terrible that you don't want to give your brother a ride to school."

That may not be the best approach.

Instead of swooning from guilt, the teen is more likely to treat the younger brother worse to prove he doesn't feel ashamed. More effectively we might say, "Your brother needs a ride to school and you have to take him. No argument."

What a beautiful statement. Short. Direct. Immediate. This is easy to understand. The teen doesn't have to consult his emotions, weigh the theological implications, contemplate his future, or philosophize over what is truth. Neither does he have to debate his moral obligation to a blossoming sibling.

Where there is indeed no other option available, the direct approach is a great communicator.

Where true guilt does exist we need to help our teen own up to his responsibility. But it is not smart to use guilt as the electric prod to move our teens from place to place.

Imagine yourself sitting in the doctor's office and hearing her say, "If you keep eating donuts for breakfast, someday you're going to look back and . . ." The doctor is totally right. Ten years from now you probably will get socked with a prescription for three or four different kinds of medicine and a diet menu designed for birds. Though true, for the moment you will probably stick with the donut diet. After all, "someday" seems like a long way off. A more effective statement from your doctor would be, "Your cholesterol is high, which results in. . . . Substitute fruit and a high-fiber cereal for breakfast."

We all respond to straightforward cause and

effect statements. Few relate to promises of far-off rewards or punishment.

Stick with short-term goals and short-term consequences. They are the best motivators.

15

Other Things Not to Say

Besides the eight things not to say to your teen, there are plenty of other questions or statements that particularly grate young people. Here are a few samples. Ask your own teen for others.

What did you learn in school today? Too specific. They hate to admit they learned anything.

I'm sick and tired . . . After they hear that one a few times it becomes tedious.

There are people starving in Africa. It's true but not a good way to motivate.

If I've told you once I've told you a thousand times. It tells the teen you are frustrated and also suggests your vocabulary has become exhausted.

What do you think I am, stupid? Teens tend to answer that in their own minds.

Are you going to wear that today? A little late to ask. Confrontational and combative.

Wait until you're older. What does that mean? How old?

What did you do at school today? Their minds immediately begin to sift through the day and look for something that you want to hear.

I thought you did a really good job (when you both know he didn't). Reduces the truth factor.

If I ever did that, my parents would have had a cow. Hard to relate to having a cow. Teen doesn't think it's clever. You're also talking about quite a generational gap.

If your friend jumped off a bridge, would you jump too? An obvious no.

It's just puppy love; you'll get over it. It shows how little you remember about young love.

This kind of thing could hurt your future. How does it affect today?

No one's going to do that and live under my roof. It's a challenge to move out. And a very limited communication tool.

I think you need an attitude adjustment. It's probably true. Simply find a new way to say it.

Well, I was a teenager once myself, you know. It's hard for the teen to imagine that, even though it is a foregone conclusion.

You just don't listen. They do listen. They don't always obey.

You're going to be the death of me yet. Teens will find it hard to take you seriously on this one.

I think you'll find it wherever you put it last. Pure sarcasm. And demeaning.

Don't ask stupid questions. A real turn-off to any kind of communication.

Be careful. Be specific. Be careful about what?

Other teens get their work done. Your child does not constitute "other teens."

Now don't make me tell you again. Don't tell them again. That's nagging.

Just remember, God is watching you. Don't pull out spiritual weapons to shoot at family problems.

I told you so. Like a dagger in the heart.

I know how you feel. Maybe. Maybe not. Everyone is different.

You don't really hate your teacher. Never reject a teen's feelings. Talk about the why's.

But yesterday you said you couldn't stand her. Teens have a right to change their minds.

It's your life. Though this statement may give your teen an independent feeling the first few times it's said, after that it becomes annoying.

Don't become super sensitive over what you say to your teen. None of the statements or questions listed above will cause any permanent damage. The goal is to improve your communication skills, not show inflexible authority.

PART THREE

Mixed Messages

"Why don't you grow up?" That's the spoken or unspoken cry of millions of parents toward their teens. We want our young people to catapult into maturity and stop acting like children.

Our insistence that they "grow up" often comes across as a series of contradictions. We want them to behave like adults, but they get into trouble for acting like adults. For a moment, try to feel the frustration a teen must experience hearing these mixed messages:

- We tell them they need to make their own decisions, but they get chewed out if we disagree with those decisions.
- They are told to act like adults but they receive few adult privileges.
- We insist that young people tell us what is going on in their lives, but they could get grounded (or worse) if they tell their parents too much.
- They are encouraged to get out and spend more time with friends, but their friends are often criticized and distrusted.

- We insist that they attend church, but they are muzzled if they criticize the church.
- We tell them "It's your life," but we want them to comply with our expectations.
- We may allow them to choose their own curfew, but they are in trouble if they exceed the "expected" curfew.
- We may desperately want our teen to begin dating, but we distrust their dates.
- Teens are prohibited from using offensive language, but we sometimes use offensive or derogatory language.
- Teens are told to behave in school, but repeatedly they hear stories of how we misbehaved in school.
- We want them to become believers, but we discourage them when they try to discuss their doubts.
- Teens are expected to neither lie nor cheat, but they see you give false information to the IRS.
- Drugs and alcohol use are condemned, but they see adults use drugs and alcohol.
- They are put down for watching too much TV, but then see Dad sit in an overstuffed chair, remote in hand.
- They are told to respect teachers and other authority figures, but we regularly degrade authority figures.

The challenge to grow up is confusing. Grow up to be like what?

Ephesians 6:4 speaks to this problem. Paul tells parents not to exasperate their children. Don't frustrate them by demanding an unreasonable standard. It would be better to encourage teens to aim for responsible behavior. The example you set provides courage. Growing up is bewildering enough without contradictory adult behavior.

Teens hear enough mixed messages out there. They should be able to receive clear messages at home.

16

Don't Take It Personally

When Owen came home at 2:00 A.M., his parents were asleep in the living room chairs. They had waited and worried as long as they could and eventually dozed off in a fitful sleep.

Awakening suddenly, they demanded to know where their sixteen-year-old son had been. He had promised he would be home by midnight, they reminded him. Not only did he not show up he hadn't bothered to call.

Owen seemed bewildered that his parents were upset. "I had car trouble," he explained, "and it took longer than I expected to figure out what was wrong. Can't you have more faith in me?"

Frustrated, his mother wailed the common aching-parent question, "How could you do this to us?"

Understandably, Owen's parents were hurt. They had trusted him with a midnight curfew and were deeply hurt by the fact that their son did not at least call and explain why he would be late. Both felt let down, betrayed. His lack of consideration had scared them and caused them to imagine the worst and worry into the wee hours of the morning.

"You don't treat the people you love in such a thoughtless manner," they accused.

But, on the contrary, all too frequently we treat the people we love carelessly. The fact that this happens doesn't mean we don't love each other. It is simply an indication that we don't think through the effect of our actions on others.

Possibly (just possibly) teens are even less careful than adults about maintaining good relationships. They think they can be thoughtless once in a while and the person they love will be understanding. Teens are often shocked to hear that the person is hurt.

The insensitivity of a teenager isn't right, but it just might be there.

Why We Take It Personally

When a teen lets us down we feel like he or she drew an arrow in a bow, took aim, and shot it directly into our heart. That's certainly half true. An arrow pierced our heart. But usually the teen did not aim it at his or her parents. Teens shoot off arrows regularly and indiscriminately. Some arrows hit their parents while other arrows hit their friends, teachers, or coaches.

The arrow hit you personally. It hurt personally. But likely, the arrow was not aimed with the intention of hurting you.

There may be an occasion when a teen intentionally and with malice or forethought tries to hurt a parent. They are capable of being vindictive, just like anyone else. But most of the time, that personal injury you received from your teenager was not intentional.

Try to analyze the situation. If your teen puts antifreeze in your coffeepot, you need to look into what he was trying to accomplish. There may be a message there.

On the other hand, the teen who rushes out in the morning leaving the bathroom a wreck is probably not trying to torture his parents.

The Real Crime

The problem that most parents face with their teens is thoughtlessness. This is a habit that needs to be overcome. All of us need to mature beyond that point. But thoughtlessness is not an intentional affront.

Why are teens so thoughtless? We could list a few reasons:

- Their hormones are swirling.
- They lack experience.
- They are drowning in their own problems.
- They need more maturity.
- They tend to be self-centered.
- They aren't aware of others' feelings.

With each individual the causes may differ. And in some cases a teen handles these obstacles extremely well and is consistently thoughtful.

Is there anything on the above list that is totally foreign to your experience with teenagers? Is there anything on the list that was not true of yourself as a teen?

Since lack of forethought is a major issue in the case of most teens, we should address that concern. If we muddle the issue by wallowing in our personal injuries, we lose the larger picture.

Teens need to be confronted about inconsiderate thoughtlessness that repeats itself. We need to look them in the eye and say, "How do you think people feel when you don't call? (Keep your promises ... Put things back where they belong ... Show up on time, etc.)."

A major goal of parenting is to teach our children to be considerate of others.

"But the wisdom that comes from heaven is first of all pure; then peace-loving, considerate, submissive, full of mercy and good fruit, impartial and sincere" (James 3:17).

Along with driver's training, personal grooming, and lawn mower maintenance, we need to teach consideration. First by example. Second by constant reminders.

Instead of confronting the issue of thoughtlessness, too many parents act wounded. They go to bed and pout because junior let them down. They refuse to talk, or they watch television in a separate room. They tell their relatives what a thoughtless, inconsiderate misfit they have raised.

You may be wounded; but you are wasting time licking your sores. Rise up to the actual problem. Call your teen back to consideration.

The Right to Feel Hurt

If someone accidently shoots you in the foot, you have every right to feel pain. Only a nitwit would suggest that stray bullets don't hurt. But you must admit you react quite differently to intentional and unintentional injury.

Children have a right to feel and so do parents.

Nothing is gained by denying our emotions. It hurts. You are angry. And you have every right to express that. Parental pain is real.

But if we want to help our teen, we must also address the larger issue. Not only did she hurt you but she hurts other people with thoughtless behavior as well.

Confront teens about their insensitive behavior toward other human beings. Challenge their self-centered attitude. Make them aware that they hurt people—and not just their parents.

Recently a young man in New York City became angry at the police and threw a thirty-pound bucket off a roof. The bucket hit and killed a policeman on the street below.

In jail the youth insisted, "I didn't mean to injure anyone. It was an act of frustration."

Whatever his intentions, his action did kill someone, and now many lives are affected by what may have been merely a thoughtless deed.

Teens who don't care how they affect others need to be called back to reality. They need to be told eye to eye that their random arrows do pierce people.

A teenager was told that he was hurting his mother by his delinquent behavior. His reply was, "That's her problem. She shouldn't take it so personally."

Many young people think they are absolved of responsibility. If they get drunk, they believe the people who love them shouldn't take it so seriously. They need to be reminded of the ripple effect. Whether it changes their behavior or not, they need to be told. And told again.

Adults need to get their personal emotions under control enough to address the real problem.

Too many teens care little about the pain they cause others. It is a known fact in boating that we are responsible for the waves we make. Teenagers need to hear that message.

17

Communication Quiz

Many parents feel uncomfortable talking to their teens. They want to communicate, but for some the experience is often uneasy, risky, even threatening. When conversation is that unpleasant, many tend to avoid any exchange with their teenagers.

In order to improve our conversational skills, it's important to ask ourselves some helpful questions. What actually happens when you try to engage your teen in a meaningful conversation? What changes can you make to increase the chances of real communication?

There are no right or wrong answers to the following questions. You don't flunk or pass. They are designed to help parents redirect their energies and create an atmosphere where sharing can take place.

1. When you start a conversation with your teen, are you uptight? Is your body tense, or are you relaxed and ready to help your teen do the same?

2. Do you lack confidence? Are you afraid that you can't hold your own in this conversation? Have you tried talking to other teens to help build your confidence?

3. Are you continually angry at your teen? Do you carry "baggage" from previous conversations? Can you feel pressure from the steam that remains stored inside? Do you need to get rid of yesterday's anger?

4. Have you made a short note to yourself? Have you listed the one or two things you want to get across? Do you have a clear understanding of where you want this conversation to go? Do you resist the temptation to wander to other subjects?

5. Do you have a hot button? If your teen mentions subjects like drugs, divorce, money, cars, boyfriends, etc., are you likely to blow up? Have you discussed this with yourself, talked to the Lord about it, and gained control over this area?

6. Do you go for your teen's hot button? When you don't know what else to say, do you throw in the explosive words or phrases that you know will set him or her off?

7. Is "needling" one of your favorite conversational ploys? Do you poke at your teen or tease to make him or her uncomfortable?

8. Do you enjoy aimless small talk? Are there times when you simply chat about small things? Does every conversation have to be heavy and driven?

9. Do you tend to dominate the conversation? Do most of your conversations turn into lectures? Are you willing to hear your teen's point of view?

10. Do you start conversations at the wrong times? Do you insist on talking when your teen is about to leave the house for school or some event?

Are you likely to show respect for their timing as well as your own?

11. How much trouble do you have with forgiveness? Are you likely to hold a grudge from last week, last month, or even last year? Can you ask God to help you wipe the slate clean?

12. Do you believe teenagers have something worthwhile to say? Have you convinced yourself that the problem is that teens talk too much and listen too little? Have you thought about your teen's assets?

13. Are you willing to spend time with your teen and let the conversation go in whatever direction he or she wants it to? Can you let your teen direct the dialogue?

14. Are you impatient? Must conversations be quick and to the point? Are you always in a hurry?

15. Are you paralyzed by the fear of "fairness"? Afraid of being labeled unfair, do you put off making decisions lest you make the wrong one? In the long run are you proving to be unfair by not making a decision?

16. Do you let your need to be loved control your conversations? Have you allowed your needs to become more important than your responsibility as a parent?

17. Are you familiar with a few sound principles of communication as they are found in the Bible?

Conversations should be

- Filled with grace (or kindness) (Colossians 4:6)
- Seasoned with salt (made palatable) (Colossians 4:6)
- Uplifting (Ephesians 4:29)
- Free from filthy language (Colossians 3:8)

- Corrective when appropriate (Proverbs 25:11–12)
- Well timed (Proverbs 15:23)
- Honest (Proverbs 24:26)
- Healing (Proverbs 16:24)
- Instructive (Proverbs 16:21)
- Free from anger (Proverbs 15:1)

Communication has been a problem throughout history, especially between parents and teenagers. Those who refuse to acknowledge this fall into weak practices and run into trouble—simply because they use the wrong approaches.

All of us have room to improve. We shouldn't let pride stop us from refurbishing our methods. Many relationships might have been salvaged if a few bad habits had been identified and corrected.

Go over these questions often and ask yourself how it's going. A few probing questions often help us to supply some good answers. Most of us know what to do. We are not lacking completely in communication skills. We merely need to remind ourselves to work at it until we see some good results.

18

Subjects of Conversation

How many parents have you heard say, "Oh, I can talk to my teen about anything"? No doubt some of those parents are being honest, but very often this statement is not true and we know it. Some subjects are easy to approach with our teens while others create instant lockjaw.

I asked many young people what subjects they found easy to discuss with their parents and which were more difficult. This is what they said.

Easy to discuss: Sports and church led the list. Facts, events, and statistics are safe areas. Dads especially seem to relate easily to sports: batting averages, passing percentages, win/loss records. It's the same way many men tend to share with each other. They feel more comfortable dealing in the abstract rather than the subjective or personal.

Church falls into the same category because it deals with events, numbers, structure, calendars, bulletins. Church is a safe subject. Spirituality may be another matter; then you're getting personal.

Borderline subjects: Some teens find the subjects of clothes and family easy to discuss. Others do not. The determining factor is how touchy those issues are between parent and teen. Clothes, for example, can be extremely personal. To the average teen they are signs of identity, freedom, self-worth, and personal expression. When parents pay for most of the teen's clothing, the teen tends to be more willing to negotiate and talk about it.

Discussions about family are productive if everyone is getting along okay, and especially if the teen does not see the extended family as intruding on his or her turf.

Hard subjects: As you probably guessed, the list of difficult subjects is long. We now enter the world of the subjective or personal. The following is not in order of importance

Girls	Makeup
Sex	Money
Drugs	Driving
Friends	Dates
Boys	Family activities
God	Report cards
Clothing	Drinking
Cars	Music, Movies, Videos

The list varies in different areas and communities, but the above represents a core of subjects that many teens have trouble discussing with their parents.

Whenever a subject is of a personal or individualistic quality, teens hesitate to bring it up with their parents. The subjects of values and moral choices are areas where most of us are apt to feel squeamish.

There are many reasons why parents and teens are uneasy around these subjects. One reason is control. Teens like to stay in control of their personal lives, and parents don't want to lose what little control they feel they have left.

Music is a prime example of this. A teen is reluctant to tell his parent what kind of music he listens to for fear he will be ridiculed or, worse, forbidden to listen to it.

Sometimes parents must take control. However, it is that threat that makes meaningful discussion less likely.

Another hindrance to open conversation about these subjects is the fear of transparency. If a parent, for example, is unwilling to open up and discuss honest feelings and beliefs about God and the Bible, the teen will also be hesitant. Many teens hide their personal beliefs for fear their parents will disapprove. They have the same reluctance about sharing with other adults.

I challenge you to go over the list of hard subjects and ask which ones you are particularly uneasy with and why. Then take the risk and broach one of the subjects with your teens.

This can be done, believe me. There was a time when I began to open up about my family of origin, then about money, sex, and being more honest about report cards. I felt it was time my teens saw their father as someone approachable on any subject. It's all part of our young people helping their parents to grow up!

19

Humor That Communicates

I can remember the day when our son became a full-fledged teenager. The telephone rang and I answered it. On the other end of the line I heard the sweetest voice this side of heaven say, "Hello, is Jim there?"

Well, I didn't know for sure, but I assured her I would try to find him.

When Jim came to the phone his mother and I sat in the living room ready to expect the usual. Normally when Jim spoke to his friends on the phone he made animal noises. He did chimpanzee sounds and monkey chatter. If he really liked the person, he would place the receiver down near his arm, put his hand under his arm, and make armpit noises.

But this time was different. Jim walked to the phone with a kind of athletic strut, picked up the phone, and said in a serious tone, "Hello, this is Jim."

We were practically blown out of our chairs. Who was this kid? We assumed he must not like the girl because he didn't even give her the armpit noise.

Sprinkled throughout the teen years are bushels of funny incidences that later become stories to tell and retell and laugh about. Not all of them are funny at the time, but looking back they are the funniest thing you can think of.

One of the saddest things to see is a parent who has lost his or her sense of humor. Their face is etched with deep concern, even when it is not warranted. You detect a constant tension in their voice. You know that whatever problems they encounter with their teen will be multiplied over because they can no longer dig up a good laugh.

It is true that some parents are indeed dealing with terrible situations. Drugs, alcohol, crime, and teen pregnancy are not laughing matters. But most of us can ferret out the brighter side to a bad situation and cut the tension.

Sometimes we need to ask the Lord to restore our sense of humor. Our funny bones become so brittle that it may take a serious spiritual transformation before we can see the happy part of parenting again. The loss of humor is a sign of spiritual death.

There is an excellent book called *Laughter in Hell*.[1] The author recounts hundreds of jokes that circulated among the Jews during World War II. Difficult times are sometimes so painful that they can only be managed with humor.

---

[1]Steve Lipman, *Laughter in Hell* (Jason Aronson, Inc., 1991).

Parenting teens isn't really a major form of persecution even if it feels that way sometimes.

One morning our daughter left for school driving our old Dodge. Within minutes we heard a horrendous noise. At the end of the block she had plowed into a small parked car. The other car folded up like a soft drink can. Fortunately, no one was hurt.

Naturally our daughter came back to the house crying and distraught. That was a proper reaction; accidents shouldn't be taken lightly. But after school the same day, we were already laughing and kidding about it. The next day she was driving again and life was back on an even keel.

The world didn't come to an end because our daughter had an accident. The wreck was a serious matter, but fortunately we were able to find a lighter side to it. By kidding her about the collision we managed to keep it within the boundaries of normal life.

Don't you think God gets more than a few chuckles from watching us? Surely you don't picture the heavenly Father exhausted from worry, keeping a bottle of antacid on hand to keep an ulcer at bay.

Some days God must laugh aloud at church committee meetings. Can't you picture God roaring when Mrs. What's-Her-Name gets all bent out of shape over the banquet centerpiece? Or when someone calls the church office complaining that the testimony of the church is ruined because of a misspelling in the bulletin?

We are so deadly serious about the wrong things. Laughter is a gift that can rescue us from some very unpleasant situations. Bringing humor to hard times is like shedding light in a dark place.

I asked a group of teenagers about lighthearted teasing and laughter. I wanted to know when it was okay to kid a teen about something, and this is what they said:

When a teen does something dumb, he doesn't want to be kidded about it right away. He needs some time to sift out his feelings and deal with his own embarrassment. But twenty-four hours later he may appreciate some good-natured teasing to ease the situation.

When someone can joke with him about the mistake he knows it was all right. No real damage was done and life will go on.

That's adding grace to a blunder or miscalculation. It may have been painful at the time; it wasn't intended to be funny. But a humorous side can often be found—later.

If the parent of a teen loses his or her sense of humor there can be harshness or condemnation. Where there is only judgment there is no hope for betterment because life is taken too seriously.

In the book of Job, Bildad says this in reference to God: "He will yet fill your mouth with laughter and your lips with shouts of joy" (8:21). This could become the parent's prayer, that God would fill our mouth with laughter so we won't lose touch with reality.

Humans are the only beings capable of laughter. Hyenas aren't really laughing; neither are chimpanzees. But people have the unique emotion that enables them to step out of their circumstances and see another perspective. It gives them the power to rise above themselves and enjoy life. If we step outside of our parent/director role and try to see a situation from our teen's point of view, we can usually see the lighter side. Our own perspective is sometimes pretty absurd.

Contrarily, a teenager is like the actor who is overwhelmed by the part he or she is playing. Many teens can't seem to step aside and see themselves because they take themselves too seriously. Everything seems deadly important.

That's why they need a parent or other adult who can laugh with them at the right time. Someone needs to show them that this is not the worst of times, even if it seems like it.

It's easy to laugh at others. The real genius is to see how ridiculous we behave sometimes. That takes maturity. And teens need to see maturity in their parents.

Don't laugh *at* a teen. Good humor makes a distinction between laughing at the person and laughing with them. A person who does something dumb is not necessarily a dumb person. Some humor is demeaning, some is releasing.

The Do's and Don'ts of Humor

1. *Don't joke about the deeply personal.* Acne, bad hair, menstrual periods, losing boyfriends or girl friends are not things about which a teen wants to be teased. These are subjects that make them feel ashamed and confused.

2. *Teasing is okay if*—enough time has elapsed to take the edge off the blunder.

3. *Don't continually tease about the same thing.* Give it a rest.

4. *Don't joke with a teen if*—your teen is not allowed to joke equally with you.

5. *Laugh with them about actions, but not about their person or personality.* Jokes about

height or weight are out. So are jokes about a teen's choice in clothing.

6. *Major on abstract humor.* Cover neutral ground—football teams, TV shows, European fashion trends, politicians.

7. *Joke; don't ridicule.* Make jokes without demeaning people.

8. *Be cautious about making jokes about a teen's friends.* Coming from you it may not be funny.

9. *Make jokes about yourself.* But not too many.

10. *Don't joke about everything.* Your teen will never take you seriously.

11. *Don't get in a rut.* Don't tell the same stories every time the family gets together.

12. *Don't ever allow a mean-spirited edge to your humor.* Teens detect this quickly.

13. *Don't try to be too humorous in front of your teen's friends.* You'll find them whispering, "That's my dad, the comedian."

14. *Don't take it personally if they don't laugh at your humor.* It may not have been funny.

15. *Repeat tasteful jokes you hear or read.* It's good to give teens an opportunity to laugh.

Humor. God gave it to us. Let's use it. But like a medicine, the doses must be administered wisely. And as "doctors" of good humor, the first rule is to do no harm.

20

The Power of Notes

Some years ago, when our son Jim was quite young, he tried his best not to let bedtime interrupt his lifestyle. Most of the time he went to his room only when we insisted, and many times he would keep the light on late.

Dutifully, I would climb the stairs to shout, scream, and threaten him, knowing full well he would not be in bed yet. "What are you doing?" I would roar. "You don't even have your pajamas on. Put that stuff away and get to bed. I don't want to have to come up here again."

Then I would huff back downstairs, face beet-red, heart pounding like a race car. Fifteen minutes later I would pull myself out of my chair and struggle up the stairs again to verbally assault my lethargic son.

One evening as I sat listening to my heart tap dance and felt my neck veins pulsate I said to myself, "Wait a minute, the wrong person is having the coronary!"

Bouncing to my feet, I hurried into the kitchen

for a piece of paper. I carefully wrote, TOMORROW EVENING JIM IS GROUNDED.

Placing the note exactly where Jim would find it the next morning, I retreated to the living room, a sinister grin on my face.

The next morning Jim bounded downstairs and paused at the dining room table, where he'd left his schoolbooks. From the other room I could hear him grumbling and snorting.

Great! I thought. *Now the right person is having the coronary.*

Words to live by. Write out this saying and post it on the refrigerator door: *It's important that the right person have the coronary.*

One of the best ways we have found to avoid short-circuiting is to write out the message we want to convey and handle it immediately. Not everyone likes this method; but if carried out under correct conditions, it is an ideal form of communication.

Here are some of the side benefits:

- You get to practice your penmanship.
- You can collect your thoughts and compose sentences without pressure.
- You can improve your teen's reading skills.
- You can clarify on paper what might be more difficult to understand if spoken under emotional duress.
- You give your teen something written that can't be misconstrued or forgotten because they didn't "hear" you.

Don't throw out this method of communication without a full and fair hearing. There are some real pluses, which should not be ignored.

1. *You can handle the matter immediately.*

Too many parents suffer for days waiting to confront their teen. Teens are seldom home at a convenient time (or decent hour). Meanwhile, we grind and mull over what needs to be said, anticipating the fatal moment when we will actually deal with the situation.

This leaves us emotionally dependent on the teen's erratic schedule. Notes allow us to set the schedule. The matter is dealt with at the moment.

2. *Notes can be carefully worded.* Most of us worry over what we will say and how we will say it. Will we choose our words carefully? Will we get overheated in the exchange and say something stupid? Or be misunderstood?

Notes can be measured. They can be rewritten if necessary. Words can be selected, rearranged.

You may even wax poetic in a note:

Early to bed,
Early to rise.
You won't get hounded
And you won't get grounded.
Please carry the trash
Out by the shed
Or you'll soon find
That your TV is dead.

3. *Notes hold teens accountable.* If your home is like most, teens tear in, around, and out again. Like field mice, they are difficult to get your hands on.

A one liner could say, "Jill, don't go out without seeing me. Love, Mom."

Or (a little stronger from Dad), "Brent, you and I will meet in the kitchen at 7:30 A.M. sharp. Dad."

Part of a teen's job is to avoid his or her parents.

(Didn't you know that?) Notes left in strategic spots help solve that problem.

4. *Notes can be enriching.* Notes don't have to always convey correction or discipline. On many occasions I have written one or two pages of praise for each of my children.

I wrote a note of praise when I wasn't getting along with one of my teenagers. I knew she wouldn't stand still and listen to me.

I've written notes just before they got married, conveying how happy I was for them and that I thought they were marrying a great person. Some things are harder to say face-to-face.

Notes and letters that praise, uplift, and encourage can become treasures to keep forever. Other times the words strike home in such a way that they will always remain a part of them.

This is why you must never write notes that are degrading, demeaning, or humiliating in any way. They will be hard to erase from the mind and heart, especially after they have been seen on paper.

5. *Notes can be pleasant surprises.* My wife leaves notes in my socks, my pockets, and even in my shorts. I learned early on never to pull a note out of my jacket pocket and try to read it with someone else around. Her messages aren't "Bring home a loaf of bread and a gallon of milk." She's a terrific communicator.

All of us like surprises. A note left in a teen's shoes, on her pillow, under his plate, is a great attitude pick-me-up. Be generous with encouraging notes no matter how rough the present road might be.

6. *Notes from afar.* Everyone likes to get mail, especially if it isn't asking for money. Young people are no exception. When a parent is away for a

few days, he or she may call home, but it's a great idea to send a card to your teenager. A card says you are thinking of them, and you care about them. It doesn't take long and it doesn't cost much money. It doesn't even have to be profound. But the thoughtfulness is appreciated, and reinforces self-worth in a young person.

By now you sense the fact that I enjoy this note thing. It has strengths and advantages that give communication an extra kick. But be prepared. Once the family learns to write, they may start to compose a few thoughts of their own.

My personal awakening came while I was speaking at a seminar in Minneapolis. I was in my hotel room getting prepared for the evening when I opened my briefcase. On top of a folder I found a piece of notebook paper. The message was in my ten-year-old daughter's handwriting:

> *Don't forget to make your bed every morning. 'Cause if I find out you didn't you will be grounded.*
> *Love,*
> *(In authority) June*

As you can probably tell, June was not shy or reluctant to express herself. I thought, *Would this fifth-grader actually call the hotel manager?* I chuckled. But not for long. I knew she was capable of calling the manager.

Every morning while I was in Minneapolis I dutifully made my bed. My neatness may have bewildered the hotel maid, but I couldn't concern myself with her problems. I had to protect myself from this note-wielding authority!

Notes That Brighten People's Lives

Years ago I wrote a letter to the editor of a local newspaper. I wanted him to know how much I appreciated his service to the local church and the community.

Soon I got a letter in return. The editor said he had seldom received a thank-you note in his forty years of reporting. Notes usually meant someone was upset, he went on to say.

My short letter brightened his day and I've never forgotten how important the written page can be.

Teens don't expect compliments from adults. When they get one they are often surprised. But everyone benefits from a positive note of communication.

21

The Verbal Atmosphere

We may know better, but sometimes we slip into ugly conversation practices. If a "mouse in the corner" could hear what is being said at your house, would he be startled?

Check the verbal atmosphere to see how comfortable or uncomfortable conversations are where you live. How do family members talk to each other?

Yes No
☐   ☐   1. Is there labeling or name calling? ("You're the dumbest kid. You don't know anything.")

☐   ☐   2. Do conversations exaggerate? ("You never do anything right. You're always lying.")

☐   ☐   3. Stone silence. (Does someone go days or weeks without talking?)

Yes No

☐ ☐ 4. Is there a great deal of shouting?

☐ ☐ 5. Is there a great amount of pouting?

☐ ☐ 6. Do conversations dwell on the past? ("You flunked math last year.")

☐ ☐ 7. Is there tension in people's voices?

☐ ☐ 8. Is there any light-hearted joking and kidding?

☐ ☐ 9. Are most conversations problem-centered?

☐ ☐ 10. Do conversations involve cursing?

☐ ☐ 11. Are conversations often concluded by someone stomping out of the room and slamming doors?

☐ ☐ 12. Is much praise being passed around?

☐ ☐ 13. Is speech sprinkled with "thank you" and "please"?

☐ ☐ 14. Is there a lot of "chewing out"?

☐ ☐ 15. Do you hear a great deal of crying?

☐ ☐ 16. Do conversations often turn into arguments?

☐ ☐ 17. Are there a lot of threats? ("If you don't, you're grounded.")

☐ ☐ 18. Is there much negotiation? ("Let's find a solution together on this.")

☐ ☐ 19. Is there a great deal of confusion? ("That's not what I thought you said.")

☐ ☐ 20. Does someone tend to shut down discussion? ("I don't want to hear about it. I don't want excuses.")

☐ ☐ 21. Is there a tendency to reject all explanations? ("And don't give me any back talk.")

Yes No

☐ ☐ 22. Is there a pattern of talking down to teens?

☐ ☐ 23. Are most praises followed by criticism?

☐ ☐ 24. If a teen gets a 95 on a test paper, will his parents discuss the fact that he didn't get a 100?

☐ ☐ 25. Are teens listened to when they speak?

☐ ☐ 26. Do adults tend to interrupt teens while they are talking?

☐ ☐ 27. Are adults impatient and give answers before they completely hear the question or problem?

☐ ☐ 28. Are conversations a natural part of the day's activities as opposed to formal, sit-down, serious communication?

☐ ☐ 29. Do adults interrupt conversations by repeating "I know, I know"?

☐ ☐ 30. Is a parent usually smiling while he or she talks with their teen?

☐ ☐ 31. Is there much laughter?

☐ ☐ 32. Are all ages participating in conversation?

☐ ☐ 33. Is there usually kindness in speech?

As you answer the above questions with regard to your own family, what trends do you notice? In two sentences write out how you would describe the verbal atmosphere where you live.

Which areas will you begin to change in order to create a better atmosphere?

22

Top Ten Places to Talk With Teens

1. *The kitchen.* Teens like to hang out where there are two exits. They enjoy talking if they can say, "Oh, I gotta run" and quickly get out of there if the conversation takes a bad turn.

2. *A restaurant.* As long as it's a place where their friends do not hang out. (They don't want to be teased about being with a parent.) A parent should not use this occasion to correct, pump, or interrogate the teen. It should be an opportunity for relaxed, open conversation where the teen is the guide—talking about whatever he or she wishes.

3. *Riding in the car.* Especially when it is just two of you. Most of us appreciate individual attention if we aren't going to be grilled. Bring up non-threatening subjects.

4. *Family room floor.* Late at night often works best. Be willing to listen way past your bedtime.

Again, best if it's just the two of you.

5. *Pursuing a hobby.* Teens will talk while doing something together with a parent, such as baking, working on a car, shopping, or sports, as long as the parent is not too dominating. (Nothing is accomplished if the parent dominates the conversation.)

6. *Meal time.* This is one of the few times when the entire family gets together and has the chance for casual or in-depth conversation. (Try to maintain at least one meal together each day. With jobs, school, community involvement, and television viewing, the family is gradually losing this time slot.)

7. *Taking walks.* With many of us becoming more concerned about getting enough exercise, a walk provides a natural get-together. When conditions are favorable, a parent may say, "I'm taking a walk, want to go along?" The response will likely be positive.

8. *Celebrations.* After a particular accomplishment, a family might have a cake or special snack to acknowledge the teen's success. It's a great time to share on a high note. (Not all conversations have to be deep and serious.)

9. *Bedtime.* You don't read to them anymore, but a back rub can cut the tension and offer opportunity for a chat. Ask permission before entering their room.

10. *Shooting hoops—or other teen turf.* It's easy to say, "What about those Celtics this year?" or "What's your favorite new song/or group?"

Some Unfavorite Places or Times for Talk

1. *Family conferences.* These may not be popular, but if your family doesn't get together regu-

larly or "naturally," you may need to call a family conference.

2. *Offices and dens—or other parental turf.* Usually a summons to one of these places means heavy stuff is about to come down. Save it until there is no other choice.

3. *In front of friends.* Chewing out a teen with friends around is unacceptable. And parents should not expect to develop a serious conversation when their teen is with friends.

4. *Outside the home.* Front lawn confrontations might be necessary but try to avoid them. Never embarrass a teen if you can avoid it. Keep heated discussions inside except in total emergencies.

5. *At breakfast.* A teen's greatest concern in the morning is for space. It's an unproductive time for confrontation or serious debate.

Conclusion

If you have ever felt like giving up, you aren't alone. I wish I had a dollar for every time a parent has said, "That's it! I'm not talking to her anymore. What's the use in trying?"

Fortunately, most parents muster up their strength, oil their jaws, and give it another try. Nearly every parent is glad he or she made the effort to keep the communication lines open.

All of us get frustrated. Many of us feel like we have reached the end of our rope with our teenagers. We may think that's the way God feels about us from time to time. But God never gives up on us. Remember the rainbow? Every time it spreads its peacock colors across the sky, we are reminded that God has promised never to give up.

Let that knowledge be a challenge for us as parents of teenagers. You might say you'll never talk to your teen again, but tomorrow's another day. Give it a rest. Tomorrow you'll have a new perspective and new opportunity to talk to your teen—and listen.

Conversation is like light to a teen. They need it in order to grow. They can no more grow in silence than a plant can in darkness. Like photosynthesis, teenagers respond to the energy they receive from light. Parents keep supplying the light by communicating.

That's the good news. So, parents, keep trying. Keep practicing. Your teens are more likely to flourish, to be safe, to find peace with God, when you are willing to stay at the task of good communication.

Let them know you will never give up on them.

Acknowledgments

Special thanks to the families, parents, and groups of teens that have been more than willing to open their lives and share experiences with me. They often volunteered information because they wanted to help others who face similar ordeals. Most of these kind spirits will have to go unnamed.

One particular set of teens warrants special recognition. We met together regularly, and they told me what it's like to be a teen. Naturally, I couldn't use all their actual stories, but I drew on their ideas and observations. And because I wanted to find positive material, I tapped into the experiences of strong families.

Their names are: Loli Bouatic, Le Bouatic, Jana Breese, Donald Gimpel, Justin Gimpel, Charlie Janzen, Chad Oswald, Aaron Oswald, Jeff Pritner, Chris Widga, and Kevin Widga.